MONTGOMERY CLIFT

MONTGOMERY CLIFT

A Biography

by
Michelangelo Capua

McFarland & Company, Inc., Publishers
Jefferson, North Carolina, and London

Library of Congress Cataloguing-in-Publication Data

Capua, Michelangelo, 1966–
    Montgomery Clift : a biography / by Michelangelo Capua.
       p.   cm.
    Includes bibliographical references and index.

    ISBN-13: 978-0-7864-1432-1
    (softcover : 50# alkaline paper) ∞

    1. Clift, Montgomery.   2. Motion picture actors and actresses—
United States—Biography.   I. Title.
PN2287.C545   C37   2002
791.43'028'092 — dc21   2002013182

British Library cataloguing data are available

Manufactured in the United States of America

*McFarland & Company, Inc., Publishers
  Box 611, Jefferson, North Carolina 28640
    www.mcfarlandpub.com*

Contents

Preface

Why Montgomery Clift? First and foremost, for his vulnerability, and for a life radically different from other film stars and incommensurable with the Hollywood lifestyle. In recent years Monty (as Clift was called) has been largely forgotten. Not too long ago, at the peak of his career in the 1950's, he was idolized as a symbol (despite his reserve) of a talented, rebellious generation of movie stars. Had he died in the devastating car accident, which irreparably disfigured not only his face but also his future, he would have been elevated to the status of a mythical figure, such as James Dean and Marilyn Monroe. Monty's story is the story of triumph but also of a complex, morose personality. His acting merged the personal and the professional, and his seventeen movies accordingly exhibit both a superb craft and an extraordinary sensitivity.

I have benefited from the help of many informants and institutions, and am indebted to friends for their assistance and support without which the completion of this project was inconceivable. I would like to thank: Pier Maria Allolio, the late Ben Bagley, Patricia Bosworth for her biography *Montgomery Clift*, Andreas L. Brown of Gotham Bookstore, New York, Michela Cinotti, Jim Fragale, Ken Galente, Julie Gilbert, the late Robert LaGuardia for his biography *Monty*, Frank Macfie, Timothy R. Mendelson, Lena Pepitone, Jonathan Poletti, Ezio Quarantelli, Mira Rostova, Walter Federico Salazar, the late Marjorie Stengel, Alexandra Stonehill, Yvette Tenberge, Donald Windham, the late Fred Zinnemann, the staff of Bobst Library, New York University, the staff of New York Public Library for the Performing Arts at Lincoln Center, Museum of Television and Radio of New York, Friends of Kent State University, Yale University library, the

Rare Manuscripts Collection of the Kroch Library of the University of Cornell, the management of the Roosevelt Hotel, Hollywood, California, and Terry Geesken of the Film Still Archive Division of the Museum of Modern Art of New York.

ONE

The Little Prince

"Son, you are a natural!"
— *Sunny Clift*

"I will never have again another child in my life," screamed Ethel Clift to the midwife on October 11, 1920, after the birth of beautiful twins: Roberta and Edward Montgomery (the name of the latter was erroneously written as Edwin Montgomery on the birth certificate). This was her second pregnancy: eighteen months earlier, she had given birth to William Brooks.

Ethel, whose nickname was Sunny for her singsong voice, was married to Bill, an extraordinarily gentle and well-mannered man, who was just nominated vice president of the Omaha International Trust Bank in Nebraska. They were living at 2101 South 33rd Street in a typical middle class household.

Bill Clift, the youngest son of the president of the Supreme Court of Tennessee, grew up in a severe environment, where all the Southern moral rules were strictly observed, along with Christian precepts. The humanitarian feelings of human brotherhood would not apply, however, to people with different skin colors, as some rumors would have the Clifts involved in a sad episode of lynching in Nashville.[1]

Bill never accepted the idea of blacks and whites sitting comfortably together in the same room, and many years after when Monty brought his black secretary home to a Thanksgiving dinner, he was unable to hide his disappointment.

Monty's mother was indeed a fascinating and lively woman. She was not very tall with a small straight nose, full lips and two expressive bright eyes that bore an extraordinary resemblance to Monty's.

Due to her conservative upbringing, Sunny never emphasized her attractiveness with anything other than the simplest styles of clothing and very minimal make-up. She had the biggest influence on her three children's lives, and played a particularly key role in Monty's. "He always thought of his father as sort of weak and helpless compared to his mother," his friend actor William (Billy) Le Massena recalled.[2]

The intricate events of Sunny's existence could easily be the inspiration for a soap opera, having as its main plot her endless love for her children and her obsessive desire to see them happy and fulfilled against all odds.

Sunny was born in 1888, the result of an illegitimate relationship. Her natural father was Woodbury Blair, Montgomery Blair's son, and the nephew of President Lincoln's personal secretary. The Blairs were one of the leading families in nineteenth-century Washington's social and political scenes. Their residence, the "Blair House," always compared to the White House, hosted some of the most important politicians of the time.

Maria Anderson was Sunny's mother; she was the daughter of Colonel Robert Anderson, who had led Union forces to Fort Sumter during the Civil War. The Andersons were also a prominent family from the area (Washington, D.C./Maryland) owning the Silverspring, one of the largest estates in that region. The reasons why the Blairs and the Andersons forbade the marriage of their son with Maria are still unknown.

Eliza Anderson, Maria's mother, despite the fact that her daughter was pregnant, voided the marriage that was celebrated in secret, and forced Maria to move with her sister Sophie to Philadelphia, in order to take her away from Woodbury. Once the baby was born, it was given to a friend: Doctor Edward Montgomery (after whom Monty was named), who delivered the child and kept the secret of the real identity of Sunny's parents.

"Sophie and Frank Adams" were listed as fictional parents on her birth certificate, a document that did not even give her a last name. For one year Doctor Montgomery personally took care of the baby; then he arranged to have her adopted by a couple from Germantown, Maryland: the Foggs.

Very little is known about her childhood and her adoptive parents; Charles Fogg was vice-president of a steel mill and was an alcoholic. Sunny was raised with the best education. Thanks to the continuous support of Doctor Montgomery, she took piano as well as singing and French lessons. Just before she attended Cornell University, Doctor Montgomery told her the truth about her adoption. The disclosure shocked her so deeply that the desire to be officially recognized by her real family quickly became an obsession. In fact, all her energy was spent, from that moment till the end of her days, on becoming part of the Andersons again.

Bill and Sunny met at Cornell in the fall of 1910. She was one of the most popular

Left: William Brook Clift, Sr., in his Cornell University yearbook, class of 1910 (Division of Rare and Manuscript Collections, Carl A. Kroch Library, Cornell University). *Right:* Ethel "Sunny" Fogg in her Cornell University yearbook class of 1913 (Division of Rare and Manuscript Collections, Carl A. Kroch Library, Cornell University).

girls on campus. All the guys were attracted to her strong personality, including Bill, who could not resist her charm. They kept dating once he graduated, getting engaged shortly after when Sunny got her degree. They went together for the first time to visit Bill's parents in Chattanooga, Tennessee. The meeting was a big mistake. The Clifts did not like her at all, since she was an orphan and a Quaker. Although the engagement seemed almost broken off, Bill was still determined to carry out his intentions: to marry her with or without the blessing of his parents.

Over the next four years, Bill changed jobs often, moving from Mississippi to Kansas, from New York to Nebraska, working tirelessly for up to fourteen hours a day. With Sunny's pregnancy, she clearly told her husband that all her children would be raised as true Anderson-Blairs, making it crystal clear from the outset that she would give all of herself in order for them not to need anything; in turn, she expected the same thing from him. The early years of Monty's life were loving and happy. While Bill satisfied all his wife's wishes, Sunny's control was absolute, trying to make her dreams come true through the children.

To avoid the summer heat in Omaha, she would bring them to New England, accompanied by Emma Wilke, a nanny, who would always follow the Clifts, even during the hard times of the recession. Emma was a hefty and taciturn woman from Chicago. She saw Brooks born in the hospital, where she was working as a nurse, and she got particularly attached to him, taking care of him until the day he left for Harvard.

In 1925 Bill left the Omaha National Trust Bank and started working as an investment banker at the New York Stock Exchange for Ames, Emmeric & Company. He would spend very little time with the children, since he was often away for business while Sunny traveled endlessly back and forth with the children.

Shortly after moving to New York, Bill sailed to Bermuda to rent a house for his family. On the boat, he met Maria Sermolino with whom he started an affair during the long periods of his wife's absence.[3]

Their secret encounters were held in Sermolino's apartment in the Village. In the same year, during the holidays in Bermuda, Sunny heard from Dr. Montgomery that her real mother had just died. The news intensified the research about her family. Finally, after multiple attempts she found her Aunt Sophie Anderson at the Wyoming Hotel in Washington, D.C. Sunny sent her tons of letters and eventually got an answer. Her excitement was incredible, because all of a sudden her life's dream was close to coming true. The old, bizarre lady, who politely welcomed her, unveiled to Sunny that Woodbury was never told of the birth of his own child. She asked her to meet with the children and as soon as she looked at Monty, she was astonished by his amazing resemblance to his grandfather. When Sunny expressed her wish to be finally recognized by the Andersons, hoping to find in her aunt an ally, the old lady suddenly changed her behavior and firmly refused to give any help. She just advised her to take the three kids overseas for at least two years, so they could be educated under the influence of the European culture, become fluent in French and German and refine their manners. Upon their return, Miss Anderson would organize a special evening in Washington. For the occasion they would be officially introduced as a part of the family. Now the most difficult task for Sunny was making Bill accept an expensive and long trip to Europe.

Later Brooks Clift stated that the Anderson story was only "an excuse from his mother in order to continue to travel and that his father would have done anything in the world to please Mother all the time, that's why they never argued."[4]

In May 1928 Sunny sailed with the children and Wilke on the Isle-de-France, a luxurious cruise boat, starting a nine-month cultural journey through Europe. In the meantime Bill was in Chicago, where they had recently moved, trying to work as much as he could to provide his wife with the high-style life that she could not give up. During the ocean crossing the kids were the object of curiosity amongst the passengers (actor Buster Keaton was one of them); they were all amused by their extraordinary appearance, which made it difficult to recognize their sex, due to their androgynous look and the triplet-like outfits. Sunny only allowed them to wear short pants and white shirts and to have the same bob haircut.

Towards the end of the cruise, something happened that was to have direct physical and psychological consequences for Monty throughout his life. While he was playing in the ship's swimming pool, a friend held him under the water for long time; in the desperate attempt to reach the surface, a gland in his neck burst, causing an abscess in his ear, which led to a high fever. Monty was immediately taken to the emergency room and once they arrived in France, he was transferred to a hospital in Paris. Sunny was extremely worried and, not trusting French doctors, went to the American Embassy to try to find a better solution. There, she was referred to a famous specialist in Munich. So, right away she left for Germany, traveling with an unconscious Monty.

Finally, after a long operation Monty had to stay still in bed for weeks with a cast around his waist waiting for the gland to heal. Monty was not even eight years old, and the operation left him with a deep scar on the left side of his neck that is still visible in photographs and in the movies he shot in the future. Sunny blamed the doctor for cutting too deep, almost disfiguring her son.

At the end of the summer of 1928 the education of the children began in Paris with theater, ballet, opera and museums. Brooks, Roberta (Ethel now, because her mother changed her name, after quarreling with the relative after whom Roberta had originally been named) and Monty were all dragged to numerous cultural and artistic events held in the French capital. Every day in their suite in the Hotel de Crillon, they were tutored in all subjects in French by a private teacher, and at night, when they were not going out, they would listen to their mother's voice reading the classics of French literature. Quickly an artistic sensitivity started to grow in Monty; often he was moved simply by looking at a work of art or by listening to a musical piece, demonstrating one of his personal traits. From Paris they traveled to Montreux in Switzerland. From here they took many trips, in particular to Geneva and to the Alps.

After Christmas, Sunny rented an entire floor of a magnificent villa in Saint Moritz Champfler. Monty spent the holidays trying skiing with his siblings and cultivating the interests that his mother raised him with since he was a child: the music of Mozart and Beethoven and books by Proust and Joyce. It is not a coincidence that during that winter Monty appeared in his first "artistic" production, *The Conversion of King Clovis,* whose religious conversion helped Christian religion to spread amongst the Franks between the fifth and sixth centuries. Monty acted in the play and helped his brother and sister to make crepe paper costumes and crowns, taking care of even the smallest details. The show was performed in the Saint Moritz villa in front of his tutor, Mr. Helman.

During their stay in Switzerland, the three Clift children made friends with Kate Billings, an American geologist and a wonderful storyteller. The kids were amazed and entertained by her African travel experiences. Suddenly, afternoons went by quickly and their fantasies were nourished by exotic images. But the friendship did not last long. Sunny got tired of Kate and using the excuse that Billings' company was not appropriate for her children, she asked her not to see them anymore.

Then from Saint Moritz they reached Vevey, where Monty met a new friend, Edward Foote, a boy of his same age, on holiday with his grandparents. Sunny found out all the information about Foote's family background directly from Edward's grandmother, who was very amused by this lady who seemed not to know the basic rules of good manners. Even though Edward found Monty conceited and self-involved, he stayed in touch with him for long time, that is, until Monty became a star.[5]

After nine months, the family came back to Chicago where they found a completely different world from the one they knew in Europe. The children's cosmopolitan experiences, their refined manners, their elegant way of dressing and their vocabulary full of French and German expressions made them appear snobbish and aloof to their peers.

As Brooks remembered with irony in an interview, their lighter and faster French bicycles saved them more than once from their schoolmates, who hated them for their pretentious manners. Brooks also recalled that he frequently begged his mother — in vain — to allow him to wear long pants and change his hair cut. But when Sunny understood how dangerous the situation for her children could be, she pulled them out of school and hired a new tutor.

The following winter they went back to Saint Moritz to polish up their etiquette. Monty was required to practice the piano seriously, and Brooks, the violin. But the cozy bubble where the children were living, made of beautiful readings, long walks outdoors, exercise and everything their thoughtful mother tried to organize for them, burst when Bill very anxiously called them back to Chicago on account of the Wall Street crash.

Sunny was very annoyed by the idea of returning, but without wasting any time, organized a trip to Washington to visit her aunt Sophie. Once again the old lady refused to introduce her and the children to the Andersons, considering them not ready for the standards of her family.

Mortified, but still full of hope, Sunny decided once again to leave for Germany, infuriating Bill because he could not afford another expensive trip for his family. He was only able to postpone the journey for a couple of months. In May 1931 the liner *Leviathan* docked in Germany and the Clifts (without the head of the family) stayed at the Bristol, one of the best hotels in Berlin, then went on to Munich, Vienna and Salzburg. Coming home was a sad experience: the antiques in the house had been auctioned off and sold. The Clifts were forced to move from their huge Highland Park house in Chicago, to a small apartment on West Ninth Street in the Village in New York.

Sunny, strong as usual, persisted in behaving with her children as if they were still living the high life: serving meals with sterling silverware and sleeping on silk sheets, always careful that proper manners were respected. She got two jobs, as a secretary at the Mount Sinai Hospital by day and as a cleaning lady at the Forty-Second Street Public Library by night. On the other hand, Bill lost his job and fell into depression, with his investments now worth nothing; his future looked completely dark. The only person who tried to encourage and push him was his wife; she eventually convinced him to change professions and accept a position as an insurance policy salesman.

As an adult Monty tended to avoid the subject of his childhood both with his friends and with journalists on the rare occasions that he granted them interviews during his career. In an article for *McCall's* magazine in 1957 he stated, "My childhood was hobgoblin, my parents traveled a lot…. That's all I can remember." In the same article was a quote from a close friend: "It was as if he had amnesia, when he was to talk about his childhood."[6] He said the same thing to Jesse Zunser of *Cue* magazine: "My formal education was a mess…. If I want to know something I have to go to my brother, who was a Harvard man or my sister, who went to Bryn Mawr."[7]

But if consciously his childhood memories were almost forgotten, unconsciously the experiences he had during that time were the biggest influences in his life, in the choices he made and in his artistic career.

In winter 1932, Sunny moved with the children to Sarasota, Florida, using Brooks' asthma and the fact that New York's cold weather would not be any good for him, as excuses. So, while Bill was in New York selling insurance policies, his wife along with Walter Hayward, an ex–English professor from Amherst, now the new tutor of the kids, traveled by car down to Florida. There Monty, now an adolescent, revealed his great interest for Shakespeare, declaiming speeches from *Julius Caesar* and *The Merchant of Venice.* Meantime, the strict tutoring schedule continued, but this time in the beautiful climate of Florida, under luxurious palm trees.

After studying, the three Clifts could have made friends their own age, if they would not have been so shy and suffocated by the oppressive presence of their mother. Suddenly, the state of isolation became unbearable for the youngsters. In those days, Professor Hayward turned Monty onto acting. In fact, the tutor had a friend who was organizing an amateurish theatrical production and who was looking for a twelve-year-old boy. Hayward thought that Monty could be interested in that role and Sunny did not object, so he set him up for an audition. On March 30, 1933, Monty made his debut in Rachel Crothers's comedy *As Husbands Go* (title that curiously resembled the Clifts' family events). "I would not know why I wanted to act, but someone said it had to do with competition with my sister and older brother. Anyway I got the part in *As Husbands Go*."[8]

Sunny, who prompted her son with his lines during rehearsals, told him after the opening with tears in her eyes: "Son, you are a natural!"

In winter 1933 they moved into a small apartment building called "The Chateau" in Jackson Heights, Queens. Bill was very skeptical about the possibility of an artistic career for his son, but Monty, who loved acting on stage in Sarasota, kept talking about it seriously.

While Brooks was sent to Friends School in Germantown, Pennsylvania, to prepare himself for Harvard, Ethel was enrolled at the Dalton School in New York. Monty instead, started his training for stage acting. After his daily tutoring sessions, he was going around with his mother to all the agents and auditions. Sunny signed him with New York-based John Robert Power's modeling agency; there he landed many profitable jobs, including ads for Steinway pianos and one for Arrow shirts.

In the following months, Sunny and Monty were inseparable. In addition to the professional commitments Monty had, they went almost every night to the theater, the opera or to the ballet. Sunny was buying him expensive gifts, such as art books, opera records and she even rented a grand piano. As soon as Monty showed a little interest in taking photographs, she bought him all the necessary equipment. Every day her attachment to him became stronger, excluding not only her husband, but also the other children who were about to move onto different paths.

The following summer, Sunny and Monty went on vacation to Sharon, Connecticut, while Bill and Brooks were on a business trip in Chile and Ethel was at a summer camp.

By a stroke of luck Monty was brought to the attention of producer Theron Bamberger, who was auditioning for a role of a thirteen-year-old boy to be part of his new production *Fly Away Home,* a comedy by Dorothy Bennet and Irving Berlin. Monty was the suggestion of a common friend of Bamberger and Bill. The producer offered him the role right away, being impressed with Monty's look and personality. Initially, he was hired without salary, just the payment of the travel expenses, since he had no previous professional experience.

Fly Away Home told the story of a father, like that of the Greek hero Ulysses, who returns home after many years of absence to find his wife remarried and his children very rebellious. Monty was cast as one of them.

The play opened on January 14, 1925, at the 48th Street Theater in New York. Critics were very enthusiastic, and the day after the *New York World Telegram* said, "Montgomery Clift handles himself with amazing poise and dexterity."[9] Actor Sheldon Leonard, who was part of the cast, became an important TV producer, and in 1959 acted again with Monty in *Suddenly Last Summer.*

Monty's twin sister Roberta "Ethel" McGinniss.

Not long after the opening Bamberger gave an interview to the *New York Times* in which he remarked that the fourteen-year-old Montgomery was both "handsome" and "intelligent" and had "a natural histrionic instinct which, if he wants to stick to the theater, should take him very far."[10] It is interesting to read the profile written in the original *Fly Away Home* playbill where the "who's who cast section" says: "Montgomery Clift has never appeared in any production [...] Only thirteen, he has lived most of his life abroad and speaks French and German fluently." The comedy, which closed in June 1935, ran for over 200 performances and it was later used as the basis for two films: *Daughter Courageous* in 1939 and *Always in My Heart* in 1942.

In order to follow their son's career more closely, Sunny and Bill moved again, this time from Jackson Heights to Manhattan onto 116 East 53rd Street. Finally travels abroad had stopped and the couple, probably for the first time since they had been married, lived together under the same roof for some months without any period of separation.

The only thing that Sunny now cared about was that Monty would leave a mark on Broadway. She was persistent in that pursuit and every agent and producer in New York knew her and her obsessive adoration for her son, making her a real character in show business.

In October 1935 Monty was cast as "the good prince Peter" in Cole Porter's musical *Jubilee,* an elegant comedy about royalty who pretend to

Monty at age 13.

be common people. Although it was performed for only sixty nights, the score of the musical became very popular in those days with the song *Begin the Beguine.*

A strange episode occurred a couple of days before the opening at the Theater Colonial in Boston. While Sunny was with Monty at Grand Central Station in New York waiting to depart by train to Boston, she was notified about an urgent personal call at a payphone. A female voice threatened to kidnap Monty if the boy remained in the production in Massachusetts. Sunny reported everything to the police, and security was enforced around the theater. Meanwhile mother and son stayed in the Footes' house in Beacon Hill. But, the threatening calls continued both at the Footes' house and at the theater. Later police finally arrested the woman responsible for them; it was only a jealous mother who wanted her own son on stage instead of Monty.

During his stay at Edward's, Monty had a hostile and cruel attitude toward his friend. Ed remembered an episode in which he stepped into the bathroom and saw Monty gazing lovingly into the mirror: "My God you are ugly!"[11] Monty said while leaving the room, referring to the acne Foote had on his face.

Suddenly, when the show had just opened on Broadway, her aunt Sophie convinced Sunny to visit her in D.C. The old lady demanded that Sunny and her daughter, Ethel, both move into Hotel Wyoming, as her guests. For the very first time Sunny did not respect her aunt's request, stating that she would have to leave her family in New York. Then Sophie tempted her with the promise of a quick recognition by the Andersons and the Blairs, but eventually the visit ended up resulting in a furious fight, in which Sophie ordered her niece to leave and disappear forever.

Sunny returned to New York in a state of shock. All of a sudden, everything she wished for herself and her children became impossible to obtain. All the years of sacrifice, the travels around Europe and the separation from her husband now seemed to be a complete waste. Although she recovered very quickly, she never gave up the idea of being recognized.

On the other hand, her aunt Sophie, when she died, left Sunny $25,000, probably feeling guilty for what had happened.

After *Jubilee* ended, Monty briefly attended the Dalton School, where his sister was a student, too. But frequent headaches and his professional duties allowed him to stay only for one year, 1936. From March 28 till May 8 of the same year, Monty took his first trip to the West Coast. He flew to Los Angeles then went on to Pasadena, where he stayed as a guest of Mary Boley, a friend of the family. After a couple of weeks he went to Arizona, where he was impressed with the wild vegetation and with the cowboy lifestyle; a photo album with over fifty pictures of this trip proves his great ability with the camera. The photographs are black and white with witty captions that were made during the journey. They include images of ordinary life: of life on the ranch or of botanical or animal subjects from the Wild West. One of those photographs was published in 1937 by a teen publication, *Saint Nicholas for Boys and Girls*, after it won the first prize in their competition.[12] Therefore, it might not be just a coincidence that the first screenplay Monty accepted was *Red River*, a western movie.

From a collection of Monty's personal papers donated by Sunny in 1969 to the Lincoln Center Performing Arts Library, it seems that in July 1934 Monty was cast as Roby in Frederick Jackson's comedy *The Road to Paradise*. No other source seems aware of it, but two receipts of payment for $40 for two weeks of work, signed both by Sunny, on behalf of Monty, and by producer Jack Linder, are proof of his appearance in the show. It was probably a little summer stock production which first played at the Alden Theater in Jamaica, Long Island, and then had a short week's run at the Brighton Beach Theater in Brooklyn.[13]

In addition to the receipts there is also a short musical score entitled "Song from the Road to Paradise." It is easy to think that Monty was cast in a role in which he was required to play and sing, using his experience from the piano and singing lessons he took during his childhood. (In 1949 in *The Heiress*, he will play the piano and sing "Plaisir d'Amour," while in 1953 he will play the bugle in *From Here to Eternity*.)

Monty was now sixteen years old and he still did not have a real friend. Sunny was starting to worry, so in June 1937 she decided to send him on vacation to Newport, Rhode Island, to the home of Ned Smith, the younger brother of Fish Smith, a friend of the family who was married to sculptor Thomas Benton.

Sunny had known the Smiths ever since she lived in Philadelphia. They were Quakers, like their own family, and this fact convinced her that they would be ideal friends for her sons. In fact, two years earlier Brooks was Smith's guest during the summer. So Bill drove him up there in his new green Buick, a car that Monty would later use until it literally fell apart.

In the beginning, Ned, who was of the same age, was a bit puzzled by Monty's personality and appearance. He was a bit too much of a "city" guy compared to himself, Ned being the outdoor and sporty type. But they eventually became very good friends.

Ned tried to encourage Monty's masculine side: every day they would go fishing, camping or sailing. He found Monty to be an excellent athlete, despite his first impression. On the other hand, Monty appreciated his host's interest in reading and discussion, and the two ended up having a lot of things in common.

"Monty influenced me in many, many ways," Smith said. "Yet I'm not sure whether the influence on me was from his mother or him, because his mother told him what to do. He was never able to be a person on his own and when he tried he lost. Monty had been brought up in a secluded way by Mrs. Clift. Most boys at [the] age of sixteen or seventeen were laying girls, but not Monty, he was reading books. Of course Monty would have sexual problems later on; he wasn't brought up to be normal."[14]

Every day in Newport Monty would receive a phone call from Sunny. He would tell her everything that he was experiencing, recounting all of the details. Mother and son also corresponded every other day.

Date: July 7, 1937

To: Mother
From: Montgomery Clift
        62 Washington Street, Newport, Rhode Island

Dear Mother
        Just received your letter. Please don't send any such a "large" sum anywhere near here. Just do me a favor. Send five ($5) dollars in cash, 'cause if I cash a check everyone knows just how much here is in it.
        I've decided not to leave here until Saturday night, which will give me all Sunday in which to "loaf." I'll also get in another little race with Viol.
        Yes, I am having "A Wonderful Time," busy doing nothing the whole day long----
        As I have received a stateroom for Saturday, I'll expect to see you Sunday "matin" at the pier. If not just let me know so I'll take a taxi right home.

Love
Monty

Date: July 1937

To: Mother
From: Montgomery Clift
        62 Washington Street, Newport, Rhode Island

I am writing you a hasty note to ask for (of all things) some money for my passage back home. I still have $4 left but it is altogether about $7 I think. The stateroom only costs $2 to reserve so it is all right if I get the rest before Friday.

Both times that Ned has raced we have come in last, but hope to do better to-morrow & Thursday.

I'll write you again before I leave.

Love Monty

*   *   *

Date: July ?, 1937

To: Mother
From: Montgomery Clift
        62 Washington Street, Newport, Rhode Island

Dear Mother:

I'll b(E) at pier 14 on Sunday. The boat docks at 7 and it would be awfully nice if someone would be here to meet the old boy. I suggest going to bed early the night before — you know, dark circles and all that----

Is it really true about my marks; i.e. what Pa said on the phone? I won't believe it until I see it in writing.

Be sure to tell Miss Brady that I'll be there for a lemon Monday, and I hope you have "*The*" Dr. Starr all lined up.

Give my love to the postman, Wilke and the folks—

Love Monty[15]

T W O

Broadway

"Look what the wind blew in!"
— *Alfred Lunt*

Monty had to wait until October 1937 before resuming his work on stage. He was cast as the youthful Lord Finch in *Yr. Obedient Husband*, a "sentimental" comedy by Horace Jackson about the life of writer Richard Steel. At the beginning of the 18th century, Steel introduced a new kind of literary journalism through his writing in the magazines the *Tatler* and the *Spectator*.

Fredric March was both the producer and the star of *Yr. Obedient Husband,* and the play marked his return to the stage after over 10 years of an extremely successful Hollywood career. At the time he was one of the highest paid stars.

The play had a long tour in the Midwest before opening on Broadway. Seventeen-year-old Monty was ridiculously escorted by his mother, who insisted upon making decisions on his behalf. In Indianapolis, Monty came down with pneumonia. Although he was determined to keep going on stage, Sunny forced him to stay in bed. On January 10, 1938, the play opened on Broadway at the completely sold out Broadhurst Theater, which was packed full of March's fans. Many show business luminaries, including Robert Sherwood, George Kaufmann and Lillian Hellman, attended the premiere. The play, though, received a negative reception and bad reviews. It closed after only one week and its producers lost thousands of dollars. Despite this, Monty was considered to be a success. The newspaper reviewers were thrilled with his performance. The *New York Herald*

16

Tribune writer Richard Watts, Jr., wrote: "There is an excellent performance in the minor role of an eager young nobleman by Montgomery Clift and [he] plays with a surprisingly successful suggestion of shyness."[1]

Shortly after that, Monty was involved in another Broadway production called *Eye on a Sparrow. Eye on a Sparrow* was written by Maxwell Selser, and it opened at the Vanderbilt Theater on May 3, 1938. It was a dull comedy about a wealthy widow who loses her fortune and cannot survive once forced to live more frugally. Monty played Philip, the widow's left-wing, radical son, and used to arrive at the theater in a limousine rented by his mother for her "little prince." The night of the opening, Monty received a warm, encouraging telegram from his sister, which he kept forever; it is now among his personal papers at the Library of Performing Arts at Lincoln Center in New York. "Darling I adore you with fervent tenderness. I wish you fame, success and greatest happiness. Your twin."[2] The show was a complete fiasco. After the first wave of terrible reviews, the director, Antoinette Perry (after whom the Tony Awards were later named), refused to have her name on the credits and, instead used the male pseudonym, John M. Worth.

Meantime, Bill Clift had finally overcome a bad period of depression. He started to work on Wall Street again for the stock exchange firm Tucker Anthony & RR. Drey. When Monty was home, he spent all his time locked in his room. There he read voraciously, driven by the desire to become more cultured and to emulate his brother who was now in college.

During this time he also kept a journal in which he noted the typical thoughts of an unhappy adolescent. He also copied quotes by famous poets or writers (like one by Irish playwright Sean O'Casey to the actor Hume Cronyn: "The theater is no place for a man who bleeds easily" or aphorisms like: "Vanity and pride work in inverse proportions" and "Poise without a point becomes self indulgence").

Six weeks later when *Eye on the Sparrow* closed, Monty was free to participate in *The Wind and the Rain,* a summer stock production in Millbrook, New York, from July 25 to July 30. Future star Celeste Holmes (she will become popular in 1950's with *All About Eve* and *High Society,* and win an Academy Award in Elia Kazan's *Gentlemen's Agreement*) was cast as Monty's love interest in this play. Although the last three plays in which Monty acted were not very successful, his talent and his reputation reached director and producer David O. Selznick, who wanted to audition him for the starring role in his next film *The Adventures of Tom Sawyer.* Due to a bad acne problem, however, Monty was forced to stay home at the last minute. The movie ended up being a flop and Selznick lost over three hundred thousand dollars.

By this time, Monty's behavior was changing. His boldness and child-ish superficiality were now replaced with a complicated sensitivity that was soon transformed into insecurity and solitude. This was a very important year for Monty because he was cast in the role of young André Brisac in *Dame Nature*, a play written by French playwright André Birabeau. For the first time he was cast in a role that required more advanced skills in the technique of acting. Up to this point Monty had more or less just played himself, but now he had to create and act as a totally different character. The farce told the story of two innocent fifteen-year-olds who unwittingly conceive a child. The subject was very controversial at that time and con-tained an imaginative opening scene in which the two youngsters admit that they have slept together and that they have done "something" that they have both forgotten quickly, without understanding the meaning. *Dame Nature* allowed Monty to taste his first glimpse of celebrity. His name appeared in big, bright letters above the title of the Broadway play. Years later, Brooks Clift stated that it was the first time that he seriously thought his brother had "a future as an actor of real talent."[3] The critics' reception was quite tepid and discordant, and not at all what the director and producers had expected. Despite the reviews, many celebrities like Orson Wells, Elia Kazan and producer Guthrie McClintic went to Monty's dressing room to congratulate him on his performance.

The opening of the play took place in Manhattan on September 26, 1938, the same day Hitler invaded Czechoslovakia. The news cast a shadow on the performance, which appeared frivolous and irrelevant compared to the events that were happening in Europe. Producer Laurence Langner recalls: "During the intermissions, I and others in the audience rushed down on 45th Street to Times Square where we could see the horrible news of doom and destruction traveling in electric lights on the sign around New York Times Building. Needless to say, our insubstantial comedy died in front of our eyes."[4] And director Worthington Miner added: "The stomp of Storm Troopers' boots drowned out the fragile voices of two teenage children in love."[5]

During the rehearsals in New York, Monty became friends with Mor-gan James who was playing Batton, André's best friend. James was two years older than Monty and was the son of a rich and extremely successful New York physician. He introduced him to Diana Barrymore, an eighteen-year-old debutante on whom Monty developed a crush, and he introduced him to the world of New York high society. They attended events such as a party at the Ritz Carlton Hotel given by Brenda Frazier, another debutante belong-ing to a very well-known family. Morgan contributed to the awakening of his friend's sleeping sexuality by taking him to New Jersey burlesque shows.

Onslow Stevens, Jessie Royce Landis and an eighteen-year-old Monty, in the Broadway play *Dame Nature*, 1938.

Those first experiences helped the still virginal 18-year-old Monty to slowly part from his mother, who was still in charge of arranging his life. In fact, she suddenly showed up one day during the running of the show in Westport, Connecticut, and shared a bedroom with her son, surprising all the members of the company.

That year with Morgan, Monty changed enormously. New horizons opened up, and he realized that art was his life and his life was art. Perhaps it was the stories that Morgan told him about the incredible things he did to prepare for roles.[6] Finally, Monty understood that it was now time to seize each of the possibilities that came knocking at his door; he needed to be willing to take some risks, as well.

During the spring of that year, Monty assisted with the rehearsal of the musical *Everywhere I Roam*, where he got to know the young conductor Lehman Engel, a chubby, cultivated gay man. He slightly resembled Monty's father, and perhaps this was the first case of noticeable paternal figure substitution in his life. This same type of friendship happens again when Monty meets playwright Thornton Wilder, and again when he meets psychologist William Silverberg. These three were all educated, gay men and they were each willing to help him escape from the intrusive presence of his mother. During a rehearsal visit, Monty took some photographs, one of which was later published in the magazine *Theatre Arts*.[7]

In his autobiography, Engel remembers his first meeting with Monty: "During the dress rehearsals of *Everywhere I Roam*, the choreographer Felicia Sorel brought a young actor to the theater who wanted to take photographs. He was nineteen and his name was Montgomery Clift. After extensive picture-taking, Felicia invited Monty to join us for tea. I had never met so lively and vital a boy. He was interested in music, painting, photographs, had studied acting with a variety of teachers, spoke several languages fluently, and was an avid reader and theatergoer."[8]

A few weeks later, Monty showed up at a lecture the musician gave in Stamford, Connecticut. They returned to New York together on the same train, and this was the start of a long friendship. For several years they went to the theatre and to museums, and took trips together. "He made everything seem so exciting," Engel wrote. "Once he called me early in the morning. 'Mon Vieux!' (his frequent term to address me), 'there's a Blake exhibit in Philadelphia. Why don't we go?'"[9]

In those months Monty appeared in *The Mother*, a drama by Karel Capek. The star of the play was legendary Russian actress Alla Nazimova, one of the most famous divas of the silent screen, and for a long time Rudolph Valentino's rival for popularity. Nazimova was well known in show business, not only for her charismatic presence, but also because of the many rumors about her ambiguous sexuality.

The Mother is set in Czechoslovakia and its central character is a woman who sees three of her four sons die in the war. When the enemies invade her homeland, she puts aside her hatred of violence and sends her remaining child, played by Monty, to fight for the country. In Richmond, as in Washington, the newspapers wrote that the audience applauded Nazimova, but not the show, and they praised Monty's performance. The opening night at the Lyceum Theater in New York, he sent a note to his costar: "Mummy darling, being Tony to your Mother has meant more than anything in the world. Merci et bonne chance. Monty."[10] The *New York World Telegram* wrote in its review: "Montgomery Clift has the doubtful honor of playing a prominent part in the Capek show. This is too bad, because he is really an excellent young actor, needing only a motherly hand to guide him."[11]

In July 1939, Monty appeared in a TV broadcast of Noel Coward's play *Hay Fever* for NBC-TV. He played the youngest child of the Bliss family and it was one of his rare appearances on video. When the show was broadcast, Monty was on holiday in Mexico with his friend Engel, who decided to go to Cuernavaca to rest and to look for inspiration for his new musical composition. Almost broke, Engel booked the cheapest accommodation on an old tanker, the *Orizaba*. Sunny, informed about the trip, asked if her son could go along with him. Engel was very enthusiastic about the request, so she reserved the only available suite on the boat.

The cabin had a private bathroom with a shower, a luxury that Lehman could not afford to have even in his own New York apartment. Sunny filled it with flowers, candies, books and liquor in order to make that journey seem like a dream.

They stayed at the Hotel Marik, sharing a little bungalow next to the swimming pool inside the hotel orchid garden. Lehman was old friends with the movie star John Garfield and his wife Robbie. The couple was in nearby Mexico City to promote Garfield's last film, *Juarez.* The strong headaches brought on by the high altitude of the Mexican capital and the terrible diarrhea brought on by the lack of clean drinking water persuaded the Garfields, under invitation of Lehman, to move to the Marik. The couple was so enchanted by the natural local beauty that they decided to postpone their departure.

At the beginning, Monty and John seemed uncomfortable together, perhaps because of their different backgrounds, but they got along well and they spent nice days visiting Cuernavaca's surroundings. They admired the beauty of nature and of architectural masterpieces like the cathedral in Taxco. When the Garfields decided to go back to Los Angeles, Monty and Engel took them to Acapulco which in those days had only one, old hotel by the cliff; the next day after saying goodbye to their friends, they flew back to Mexico City. The little plane was so old and shaky and the wind was so strong that it took over five hours to reach their destination instead of the usual 45 minutes. This virtually scared the two passengers to death.

Upon arrival, Monty got seriously sick and was rushed back to New York where a strong amoebic dysentery was diagnosed. This illness would affect him for the rest of his life and often forced him to travel to Tulane Medical Center's Ochsnec Clinic in New Orleans which specialized in the treatment of this illness.

The "affair" between Monty and Engel was on the rocks; Lehman realized that "this darling boy" would never grow up and knew that what he needed was a father figure substitute. Their close friendship slowly faded, and they rarely saw each other again.[12]

Monty started a new, separate life far from his mother. In order to avoid his mother's intrusive curiosity, he seldom brought home his friends. She later stated, "I knew right away he was addicted to little boys. It shocked me and I told him so, and I said it would weaken him artistically. His father was furious. 'How can a son of mine stoop to this?' he asked. He said I was entirely too gentle about the matter!"[13]

As time passed, Monty slept with both men and women, hoping to discover his own sexual preferences. Sex always caused interior conflict, which tormented him all his life. His sensitivity was unable to justify completely his complicated sexual behavior. Brooks often mentioned that his brother was bisexual, and said that he even got two girls pregnant (both of them were later forced to get abortions) and that it was only in the later years of his life that he became homosexual. He theorized that this change was due to strong disappointments he suffered.[14]

Monty's almost exclusively gay predilections were confirmed by a taped telephone conversation between Sunny and Brooks after Monty's death, in which the mother talks with no problem about her son's homosexuality. "Monty was a homosexual very early! I think he was about twelve or thirteen years old." And Brooks in vain tries to convince her that his brother was bisexual.[15]

Monty was very worried about his health problems and he started to take all kinds of pills to soothe his upset stomach. His pockets were always filled with them and he learned every possible thing about those types of medications. He monitored his diet, eating only raw steaks and exclusively drinking milk, but he held onto a fear of gaining too much weight. In August 1939, after a short vacation in Maine with Ned Smith, Monty was cast in the comedy *Life with Father,* which would go on to became one of the biggest of all time on Broadway, lasting for more than 3000 performances.

Monty had his hair curled and dyed red for the part and started to rehearse, but was fired after only five days. The reasons why he was canned are not very clear. Some think that he was not convincing for the role because his look was not ordinary enough in the director's opinion. Others think that it was because the tone of his voice was not right for a part in a comedy. Monty became depressed and thought that his acting was no longer convincing. He called his friend Engel, who tried to comfort him by telling him that it was normal to be fired at least once in a lifetime and that it was just another part of show business.

A couple of months later, the situation turned back to his favor. In fact, if he had not been fired from *Life with Father,* the Lunts would not have been able to cast him in their new production of *There Shall Be No Night,* written by Robert Sherwood. For Monty, it would prove to be the most important experience on stage ever. Alfred Lunt and Lynn Fontanne were the major figures on Broadway at the time and they were Monty's idols.

There Shall Be No Night was inspired by a Christmas radio program and it was broadcast by Helsinki's CBS Radio. It was made to remind the American people that a Soviet invasion of any free country, in this specific case Finland, was a terrible threat to all democracies. Alfred Lunt had believed in "the theater as a place to express high ideals and this was a play that said something that had to be said."[16]

Billy LeMassena recalls that on the day of the audition Monty was so nervous that he drank three pots of strong tea. He arrived at the Alvin Theater like a young prince, wearing a proud expression on his face and wearing a gray flannel suit by Brooks Brothers and a pair of shiny black loafers. When it was his call, he bowed in front of Lynn and clicked his heels in a respectful greeting. Alfred Lunt just looked at him and said, "Look what the wind blew in!"[17] And Monty got the part of Erik, Lunt's son on stage. In only one week Billy LeMassena, Phillis Thaxter and Robert Downing were added to the cast.

With the Lunts' guidance Monty quickly changed from a sensitive life observer into an intense and committed actor. The couple became so attached to him that they gave him an inscribed photograph of themselves as a gift: "To Monty from your real parents." They often invited him to their apartment for dinner, or selected plays for him to read which would broaden his knowledge of dramatic literature. They encouraged him to devote his career not to money or to fame, but to performing in work of the highest quality, as they, themselves, had done.[18]

Actor Dick Van Patten, who later worked with the Lunts, remembers how much they loved Monty: "He was their favorite actor…. They raved about Montgomery Clift. They thought he was going to become a great great star because of his acting ability…. They were not very happy about the idea he wanted to make movies."[19]

Monty was fascinated by the way Alfred was acting. He started to carefully observe his mannerisms and style, transforming himself into a sort of "young Lunt" with a new, particular way of speaking: intense, slightly hesitant, pronouncing some words very quickly in the middle of a sentence and others with extraneous pauses, looking deeply into the eyes of whomever was standing in front of him. Alfred was always calm and sure of his emotions, while also being very simple and down to earth. Monty's was not just an imitation, it was the result of the influence of an absolutely unique acting style just perfect for that kind of show.

In an interview in 1944, Monty stated that acting with the Lunts was an extraordinary experience. Although there were many difficulties, the couple always helped him and they were ready to deal with any doubts that he had regarding his own performance.[20] The play debuted in Providence, Rhode Island, on April 29, 1940, and opened on Broadway at the Alvin Theater, then beginning a tour from November 1940 until May 1941. The troupe performed in 46 cities and the reviews were almost all good. *New York Times* critic Brooks Atkinson wrote: "Montgomery Clift has grown up to the part of the son and plays it well."[21]

During the Broadway running of the show, Monty spent the weekends with his friend Billy LeMassena at the home of literary agent Janet Cohn in Pound Ridge in Westchester County, upstate New York. Since the end of the 1930's, Cohn's was the meeting place for new young talents in show business, in addition to many playwrights belonging to the agency of Harold Freeman, Cohn's boss. Monty and Billy rented a big converted barn just down the road from Janet's place, in order to be closer to Pound Ridge; they renamed it "Red Barn."

Sunny did not like the idea because she was left to spend the weekends alone, so she would often surprise Monty by arriving unexpectedly. Furious, Monty started to treat her badly by not paying attention to her. He had just started to live his own life and wished that his mother would understand it and leave him alone.

Billy recalled that: "Monty had become a name on Broadway already, and producers and directors were all looking out for him. And there is no doubt, this boy was an extraordinary person; he was when I first met him and he remained so, basically until his death. In those early years on Broadway ... he did not drink or smoke and it is no exaggeration to say that he had an innate, organic morality of a saint at that time. Very early on I learned that any kind of transgression that violated that friendship would hurt him tremendously and leave him helpless with emotion, [and] cruelty of any kind, whether to animals or children, just injured him. He could not cope with it. It wasn't his upbringing, it was just the genius of him."[22]

The nature of the friendship between Monty and Billy remains uncertain, but according to mutual friend and writer Donald Windham, in the beginning they were lovers.[23] According to Barney Hoskyns, Monty may have engaged in his first alcoholic drinking binge with another cast member, Richard Whorf, when *There Shall Be No Night* was touring nationally.[24]

Often Phillis Thaxter visited him at Red Barn. Thaxter was originally from Maine and was a beautiful brunette. She used to spend hours talking with Monty about everything, and they would go to the movies or to the Museum of Modern Art. When Phillis was chosen to replace Dorothy McGuire in *Claudia,* Monty hosted her in his house for a few months.

The Clifts were excited that their son was going out with such a delightful girl. Sunny quickly told everybody that Monty and Phillis were engaged. But the relationship was only platonic, as Thaxter later admitted. Although sometimes they talked about marriage, Monty told her one day that he would never marry her because "it just would not be right."[25]

He told her with such a serious and sad expression on his face that the poor girl did not have the courage to ask for further explanations. She sensed, indeed, that he also liked men and she knew that when they were not together he was leading a totally different life, one of which she was not a part. The other members of the company also suspected that Monty might be gay. He had, in fact, started an affair with a man he met at the gym. He would often hang out with him and take him to his parents' house without worrying about appearances. Even Alfred Lunt noticed something strange and warned him about how dangerous some of these behaviors could be if a rumor of this type were to spread. It is hard to say if Monty felt guilty for being gay. Certainly the fact that he was always very secretive about it proves that he did not feel very comfortable with it.

Meantime, word of his talent reached Hollywood. The big studio managers were always looking for new, emerging actors and they attended all of the Broadway shows to scout new, interesting faces to launch on the big screen. Louis B. Mayer saw *There Shall Be No Night* and wanted Monty for MGM's *Mrs. Miniver.* He offered him a seven-year contract with a weekly salary of $750. Monty refused, not only because he was pushed to do so by the Lunts, who did not like the movie industry and considered it a threat to the theater, but also to rebel against Sunny's ambitions. He knew that she would have given anything to see him in a film.

In August 1941, when *There Shall Be No Night* stopped running for summer break, Monty acted for a week in *Out of the Frying Pan,* a comedy by Francis Swarm, at the County Theater in Suffern, New York. He played Tony Dennisson, a young man living with five other aspiring actors in an apartment upstairs from a Broadway producer. They continuously try to convince him to hire them for his next show. The farce was inspired by real events that happened to the author's sister. Shortly after the tour of *There Shall Be No Night* resumed, it was suddenly shut down on December 7, 1941, when the Japanese bombed Pearl Harbor forcing the United States to join the war. Due to its controversial subject matter and setting, the American government requested the interruption of the show at once.

President Roosevelt personally asked author Robert Sherwood to suspend the performances for political reasons. The last show was held in

Rochester, Minnesota, three months before the originally scheduled closing date.

Monty benefited from the situation and took a short ski vacation with
Billy in Wisconsin. "He went to the top of a slide of a lift, sat down in the
snow in his suit and topcoat, and slid to the bottom of the slope," Billy
LeMassena said. "When he realized I was taking movies he dropped his
pants and waved happily to the camera."[26]

One week later his dysentery and colitis worsened and that spring they
became so painful that he was forced to return to New Orleans. Sunny
asked Billy to go with him and stay by his side while he was in the hospital for three weeks. Shortly afterwards Billy and Ned Smith were drafted
into the army. Monty asked to join the ski troops, but was rejected because
of his medical condition.

The previous summer Monty had met Robert (Bobby) Lewis through
Janet Cohn. Lewis had been a founding member of the Group Theater
eleven years before along with Harold Clurman, Lee Strasberg and Cheryl
Crawford. In April 1942 Lewis decided to direct an experimental production off–Broadway called *Mexican Mural* and he offered Monty a role in
the show. Lewis first read the script when it was submitted to a contest
organized by the Group Theater for new playwrights under twenty-five
years of age. Tennessee Williams had won one hundred dollars for three
one-act plays, but the top prize of five hundred dollars went to Ramon
Naya for *Mexican Mural*.[27]

Settling on a tiny auditorium on the fiftieth floor of the Chanin Building, a skyscraper at 123 East 42nd Street, the director started to select the
cast. Besides Monty, Libby Holman, Kevin McCarthy, Mira Rostova and
Billy LeMassena, who returned early from the army, were chosen for the
show. One afternoon Libby and Monty casually bumped into each other
as she was leaving the studio and he was coming in. Libby could not speak
after Monty smiled, apologized and moved away. As she later told his friend
George Lloyd: "I was burning up; just looking at him made me feel like I
would catch an incurable fever."[28] At that time Libby was 38 years old and
was a famous torch singer. In 1931 she had married millionaire tobacco
heir Zachary Reynolds Smith, who was found dead in their apartment one
year later while Libby was pregnant with his child. Apparently Reynolds was
homosexual and depressed because he had been afflicted by a temporary
case of impotence. Many do not believe that he committed suicide, but
that his wife shot him. She was even tried for murder. At the end of the
trial Libby was discharged for lack of real evidence. After a long legal bat-
tle, she obtained seven million dollars from the Reynolds estate.

When Lewis decided to put together the Group Theater and orient the production toward less commercial plays, Libby helped him financially. In the production journal dated February 1, 1942, it is written that Libby put down ten thousand dollars, a huge amount at the time, even before *Mexican Mural* was chosen (Lewis does not say if Libby's participation in the play was mandatory after her generous contribution).[29] On February 10th, the play was picked from many Lewis had read, and on March 6th Monty was asked to play a part in it.

Mexican Mural was divided into four "panels." They told the stories of various people in Vera Cruz during the Shrove Tuesday carnival. Monty played a young man eager to lead a life that was not so provincial. The play depicted the religion, superstition, poverty and desperation of Mexico. On the first day of rehearsal, Bobby told the actors to treat Libby as if she was anybody else in the company, but as soon as she showed up at the theater, nobody in the company could help but look her up and down. While rehearsals went on, lasting for over a month, Libby quickly won everybody's respect with her hard work and by refusing any special treatment.

More than one time, Libby tried to bond with Monty by inviting him for a drink, but he always shyly turned down her offers telling her "I only drink milk!" Soon the other actors in the cast noticed that "something peculiar" was going on between the two of them, without a sexual involvement or interest, at least on Monty's part. Libby was impressed not only by Monty's dramatic talent, but also by his androgynous beauty; he liked her sense of humor, her strong and bizarre intelligence and the fact she seemed to deeply understand him.

When *Mexican Mural* opened on April 27, 1942, Brooks Atkinson wrote in the *New York Times*: "It is a strange, wild evocative sketch of vital, underdisciplined civilization.... Some of the acting is excellent, especially Montgomery Clift's superlative portrait of a brooding beaten youth."[30] Later Tennessee Williams said to the same newspaper that the play was one of the best he saw that year. But altogether, the reactions to it were not enthusiastic and Robert Lewis gave up the idea of organizing a permanent theatrical company, and moved to Hollywood to act in the same movie. He returned to New York in 1946 to open the Actors Studio with Elia Kazan, where Monty briefly attended some classes.

Monty's participation in this short production was more important for his personal life than his professional life, because he met Mira Rosovskaya (later changed into Rostova), a Russian émigré, who first moved to Germany where she grew up and started a career as an actress in a Hamburg theatrical company. When Hitler rose to power, she was forced to continue her acting exclusively in a Jewish ghetto she later had to escape

Publicity shot. Late 1940s.

with her family; she then moved to New York, where she become a student of Bobby Lewis. Mira was a thin little woman who looked like the French singer Edith Piaf. She was five years older than Monty and used to address him as "my comrade." Her willing power and clever ideas as to how an artist should live and work strongly impressed Monty.

Robert Lewis recalls that in those days: "Everybody was in love with him. He was absolutely mesmerizing in the show, and off-stage, he was like Pan, an enchanter. Everybody clustered around him and talked and took photographs. But he refused to play favorites. One afternoon, he might sit with Libby and light her cigarettes, another evening he'd be with Kevin [McCarthy] and Augusta [Dabney] for dinner, but much of the time, he spent with Mira Rostova and I think that ticked Libby most of all. Libby was used to having her way around men, and yet here was this Mira Rostova with her woebegone little face out of a Kathe Kollowitz drawing, who was monopolizing Monty."[31]

Tabloids often described Mira as Monty's biggest romance, while she always stated that they never had any affair. Instead they shared a feeling of mutual devotion and respect for one other.[32] Later Mira herself would be the biggest influence in his career and would be present on the set of many of the movies that Monty shot. During a 1950 interview for the *Chicago Sunday Tribune* with Hedda Hopper, the biggest Hollywood gossip columnist, he said: "I think it would be correct to say that Mira is a very dear friend whose judgment I respect tremendously. I can depend on her for an honest opinion."[33]

Thanks to *Mexican Mural*'s experience, Monty also became very close friends with Kevin McCarthy, who remembers: "We got to be friends almost instantly, we had something in common, whether it was taste or a common taste … it was a share of some kind. And I do think it was we thought we knew better than other people how things should be done. We were egotistical … [enough] to believe that most of the things we saw were not well done, most of the acting we were asked to respect we thought not very highly of. We thought that we were better than they were and we could perform it better. That our tastes were better and therefore in some way we must assume that we were born more intelligent, more cultivated, more something! He was a remarkable person and the fact he was interested in us and liked us so much was flattering possibly to us, because he seemed the personification of 'the young prince' with all the best qualities…. He used to say 'I want to live the most fruitful life!'; it is unfortunate that in some way in the fruitfulness there was a dark fruit, a rotten fruit finally at the end."[34]

A statement that Monty repeated often, impressed Kevin because it could be a possible explanation for some of his strange behaviors: "I'd like to go deep down in the drags of life in some way like Dostoevski's "Notes from Underground" and see what that's like and then get back."[35] With the same intensity, Augusta Dabney, at the time McCarthy's wife, adds: "Monty was wonderful, it made everything feel special, every person he met. Everybody loved him."[36]

After *Mexican Mural*, Monty and the McCarthys became inseparable. A lot of malicious insinuations began to circulate, perhaps because they all frequently embraced passionately in public. But all the people close to the McCarthys knew that the attachment that the young actor had for the couple, who at the time were very much in love with each other, was generated by the sense of protection that Monty needed without involving any sexual connotation. He loved to play the part of the young, irresponsible brother while with them, and at the same time he adored going with them to cultural and social events. The trio pretentiously referred to themselves as actors belonging to the "New Wave of the American Theatre."

While unemployed, Monty spent most of the summer of 1942 on Cape Cod with Augusta, who was playing in a summer stock production of *The Pursuit of Happiness*. Her husband was in the army and visited her on and off on weekends. Augusta recalls those months as a period of great happiness, and as one of the most carefree and exciting times of her life. Her days were spent laughing and having fun with her friend who was always affectionate and helpful. On many occasions Monty would say that Gussie (the nickname he gave her) was the only girl who he could have married. In a letter he wrote to his sister Ethel he said: "Gussie is never too busy to listen to me and she has the best sense of humor. If she were free, I'd marry her tomorrow."[37] Brooks, who always believed in his brother's bisexuality, will state that Monty only loved one woman in his life: Augusta. But the fact that she was married to his best friend always stopped him from expressing his feelings to her.[38]

When he returned to New York in September, Monty was cast in Thornton Wilder's new comedy *The Skin of Our Teeth*. The director was

Turkish-born Elia Kazan, the son of a carpet merchant who had been raised in New York. He was a very determined man who was striving to make a career as a director on Broadway. Kazan was not a very open-minded or liberal person. He was the co-founder of the Group Theater with Robert Lewis and others. He did not like homosexuals and shared this opinion with a group of rebel intellectuals who gathered around drama teacher Lee Strasberg and playwright Clifford Odets. They all considered homosexuality to be evil and felt that it was a threat to the theater (although there were assuredly a huge number of gays in their group).

For Monty, accepting that role was a double challenge: not only did he need to prove his masculinity, but he also needed to show his agent, Leland Hayward, that acting the part of a naughty adolescent was not a step back in his career at a point when he could aspire to a role as a protagonist.

There are two versions as to how Monty obtained the part of Henry Antropus. Patricia Bosworth says he was helped by playwright Robert Ardrey, Kazan and Monty's mutual friend.[39] Gilbert Harrison states that Thornton Wilder wanted him after seeing him acting on stage a while before.[40]

Famous Tallulah Bankhead, Fredric and Florence March and Florence Reed were all part of the comedy's large cast. Kazan recalls in his autobiography: "Four stars, and Montgomery Clift, who was to become a star, were lined up before me. I introduced them to each other. The traditional show business embraces were not forthcoming; they nodded, smiled, waved hands, kept their distance. Monty was visibly impressed with the select company he was part of.... Florence Eldridge March chattered, straining to be believed the cordial one.... Tallulah responded with her horse's laugh and nicotine cough. When rehearsals started, [something was] immediately apparent: the tension between the Marches and Bankhead, which I'd anticipated; and it was my job daily to prevent fights between them.... The first dress rehearsal was a nightmare of hysteria. Bankhead was never quite offstage, never on time for her entrances, never anything but hateful to the other actors. Florence March was wretched and, it seemed to me, frightened: Freddie furious: Florence Reed haughty and scornful of us all: and Monty Clift awed by the minefield of temperament exploding around him."[41]

Kazan was impressed by the fact that Monty never took anyone's side. Meanwhile in California, Thornton Wilder was alerted by phone calls and letters from the director of the theater that pushed him to go to New York to personally understand the reasons of all this commotion. His sister Isabel, who would later become a very dear friend of Monty's, set up all the appointments so as not to generate further discontent between the actors, each of whom wanted to personally share their own frustrations with the playwright. Thornton was forced to secretly meet with Monty at Sardi's, after he had to listen to an annoying Tallulah, who was complaining, fighting everything and nagging everybody.[42]

Acting the part of 14-year-old Henry, Monty was capable of separating himself from all the tensions around him. He was able to concentrate on learning as much as he could from Kazan and Fredric March. The director became a paternal figure to him (as he would later be for Marlon Brando and James Dean), believing Monty was "a sexual borderline case." He encouraged his wife Molly to mother him and to try to show him the "right way."

On November 18, 1942, *The Skin of Our Teeth* opened on Broadway at Plymouth Theatre to almost unanimous acclaims from reviewers. The day after the debut, Thornton Wilder sent Monty a telegram from California : "Reports reached me you are magnificent. Thanks and best wishes."[43] The actor proudly treasured it forever.

The Skin of Our Teeth told the story, in an allegoric form, of a family trying to survive over the course of 5000 years. Many of the actors dressed up as extinct animals, wearing colorful costumes, while the stage designing was inspired from cartoons.

One month after its opening on Broadway, *The Skin of Our Teeth* was the subject of a literary controversy in an article that appeared in the Saturday Review of Literature.[44] It claimed that Wilder had borrowed the subject of the play and part of the dialogue from James Joyce's *Finnegans Wake,* accusing the playwright of plagiarism. The controversy cooled when the famous writer Edmund Wilson publicly defended Wilder, who did not pay too much attention to the polemic since he was busy in the Air Force Intelligence Division. Despite the unpleasant episode, the play won the Pulitzer Prize for best original play.

Although Monty was economically independent, he still was living with his parents. Often he would escape to Mira Rostova's studio on East 55th Street, when she was out of town on tour. He wanted to live in his own apartment, but his mother still had a very powerful influence over his life. "Why does she keep trying to control me? She will not leave me alone!" he often complained.[45]

Besides, Sunny was totally disapproving of her son's new friends. According to her, Libby Holman was a pervert, Mira Rostova an opportunist and Kevin and Augusta McCarthy were not of his class. She particularly detested Kevin because he was too proud of his Irish origins and he was an orphan. She often repeated, "What is his ancestry, his genealogical tree?"

And she told Monty not to see him again because "he was nothing, he was a nobody."[46]

That year Monty met Jeanne Levy, a pretty 21-year-old girl who was married to sports editor Fred Green, who was drafted in the Air Force and stationed in Europe at the time. Jeanne had been born in Chicago and she had been Augusta McCarthy's roommate when they both attended the American Academy of Dramatic Arts. Jeanne remembered their first meeting with great emotion:

> I had been not well, I had a miscarriage and I was staying out in the suburbs with my mother. I was very depressed and felt very lonely and I called Augusta to talk to her and she said she and Monty were together. It was Sunday afternoon, as I remember, and she said: "Can you get on the train and get in?" and I said: "Yes but I cannot walk very well. I'm weak." And she said: "That's all right, do not worry about that, Monty will help you!" So I get on the train and came in and they met me in Grand Central Station and I remember him very well, when I first saw him. He was very slim and incredibly good-looking, alive, bright with a luminous face and somehow they got me to Augusta's apartment to a four flights walk-up. I said I can't make it and he just picked me up, like a doll, and not walked but ran four floors up…. [He] was in incredible physical condition, and we talked and he was alive, funny … not funny! That's the wrong word for him, it was zest, he had a kind of mad wild, crazy way of talking and witty, very witty and the combination of the two was just sheer wonder, sheer delight. I forgot that I had lost a child, I forgot that my husband was on a plane, I forgot to worry. He became alive. He made everything alive![47]

Once she recovered, Jeanne started to go with Monty and Augusta to dinner or to the theater, becoming another inseparable friend for Monty. Even if in a platonic way she fell for him, but it is certain that they were never lovers. Monty's friendship was not a threat in any way to her marriage. As Augusta stressed: "Every girl, woman was crazy about Monty and he seemed to be in love with all of us individually. He had girlfriends but there were two or three of us, he was very fond of. We were very very close, but I do not think it was a coincidence that each of us was married, so the relationship was protected by the fact I was married and couple of other people were married. And I do not think he wanted them divorced. The protection was what made the relationship so nice."[48]

Both Augusta and Jeanne loved being in his company, but they often felt frustrated when he would disappear for a few days. Ultimately, they would meet him in the street with some dull boy. Monty never gave any explanation regarding his own disappearances or his mysterious escorts, and nobody dared talk about the possibility that he could be gay. At the time it was not an easy subject to discuss.

The following spring, Monty, due to overpowering colitis, was forced to leave the play and travel again to New Orleans for treatment. This time it seemed to work better than in the past. Upon his return to New York at the end of the summer, he received the family's car as a present from his father. He would drive the 1937 Buick up to Connecticut every weekend to visit his friend Janet Cohn. While there, he became better acquainted with Thornton Wilder, who was off from his military duties with the Air Force and often at Pond Ridge as guest of the literary agent.

In January 1944, Monty was starring in a New York revival of *Our Town* that ran on Broadway for just 24 performances. Thornton Wilder wrote the play that had been one of the biggest hits of the 1937-38 Broadway season; it is now considered a classic of the American theater.

All the reviews raved about his interpretation of George Gibbs: "First-rate performance" "superb" were some of the praises. Libby Holman was in the crowded audience on opening night. She claimed that she swooned at Monty's performance and she told a friend who was with her: "Isn't he the most beautiful youth you ever saw? I'm a cot case over that boy!"[49]

Immediately afterwards, Monty was involved in the first of three plays that would establish him as the most talented Broadway actor of his generation. The first play was Lillian Hellman's *The Searching Wind*, an indictment of America's shortsighted foreign politics during the 1920's and 1930's, when Hitler and Mussolini rose to power. Monty played Sam Hazen, the son of a diplomat who was seriously injured in the leg during the war. Cornelia Otis Skinner and Dennis King were the stars of the play, but Monty, even though he was in a supporting role, stole the show. His moving lines represented the core of the drama and with them he completely captured the audience's attention.

The Searching Wind opened on Broadway in April 1944 and toured the United States for over a year. Director Herman Shumlin did not want Monty to imitate (especially in the voice) Lunt's mannerisms and, therefore, he asked him to speak with as little accentuation as possible. During the rehearsal, Monty got along particularly well with actor Dudley Digges and with Lillian Hellman, who in her autobiography remembers how Digges was meeting early each morning with Monty to study scenes from Shakespeare, Ibsen or Chekov, anything Digges had chosen to teach him, "A gifted inexperienced young actor in his first large part."[50]

Often Monty used to entertain his colleagues backstage with funny imitations. His favorite impersonation was Charlie Chaplin in *City Lights* or his co-star Cornelia Otis Skinner, who was slightly deaf. He would impersonate her trying to understand the director's words which he whispered to her in her dressing room.[51]

During that month of rehearsals, the *New York Herald Tribune* interviewed Monty for the first time. On July 16th Irving Drutman wrote a long article in which Monty reveals that "acting with people like that, it is a remarkable experience…. It is very inhibiting at first to be on stage with them and hear them speak lines, because everything they say seems so right and everything you say after them seems so phony by contrast."[52]

Monty was photographed by John Rawlings for *Vogue* magazine. In the caption above the picture is written: "Montgomery Clift gives the best performance of the season in *The Searching Wind*, Lillian Hellman's controversial successful play."[53] Brooks cut the photograph and proudly showed it to all his friends and relatives saying that his brother was absolutely great.

Marlon Brando, who at the time was relatively unknown, was a fan of Monty's performance. Brando was acting in New York in *Truckline Café*, directed by Harold Clurman, who co-produced the show with Elia Kazan. Marlon, 20 years old, was born in Omaha, Nebraska, like Monty. He would always wear a pair of jeans and a T-shirt and was taking acting classes with Stella Adler, a very gifted teacher, who had learned the Stanislavski method in Germany. Later Monty and Marlon will end up together in the same acting class at the Actors Studio, where classes were based on the famous "Method."

Marlon Brando:

> Another friend from that era who died sadly and prematurely was Montgomery Clift. We were both from Omaha and broke into acting about the same time. We had the same agent, Edie Van Cleve, and, although he was four years older than me, we were sometimes described as rivals for the same parts. There may have been a rivalry between us—in those days I was a competitive young man determined to be the best and he was a very good actor—but I do not remember ever feeling that way about him. In my memory he was simply a friend with a tragic destiny.
>
> We met while I was in *Truckline Café*. By then Monty had been in several plays, and I was curious about how good he was and went to see him in *The Searching Wind*. He was good, and after the play I introduced myself and we went out for dinner. Since we shared a lot of similar experiences, there was a lot to talk about and we became friends, though not close ones. There was a quality about Monty that was endearing: besides a great deal of charm, he had a powerful emotional intensity, and like me, he was troubled, something I empathized with. But what troubled him wasn't evident. Later on, I went out with a girl he had dated (Ann Lincoln) and she said she thought he might be a bisexual or a homosexual, but I found it hard to believe. I never asked him and never suspected it, but if he was a homosexual, I imagine he was torn asunder by it. Whatever the reason,

he was a tortured man, and to deaden his pain he began drinking chloral hydrates and became an alcoholic.[54]

At the end of 1944, Ned Smith helped Monty to move out of his parents' Park Avenue apartment into Mira Rostova's old studio on 122 East 55th Street, which she sublet to him. Finally, Monty was able to do everything he always wanted. He could invite his friends over at any moment of the day or night and could spend all his free time talking on the phone without being bothered by his inquisitive mother.

Sunny disapproved of her son's decision to move out and accused him of abandoning his family. Monty, as friend Ben Bagley recalls, was later forced to have three different phone numbers. One of them was exclusively for his mother, so he would know when she was calling him and, therefore, could decide whether or not to answer.[55]

Living by himself allowed Monty to dress more casually and often in a shabby way, something really unusual for a movie star, as later journalists would often remark. All of this started as a form of rebellion against his conservative parents.

Then again in the role of a veteran, Monty increased his popularity on Broadway enormously by starring in Elsa Shelley's *Foxhole in the Parlor*. It was his first part as a main star on Broadway, and he received the highest salary out of all the actors in the production and had his name in big letters on the billboard outside of the theater.

The play debuted on May 23, 1945, and toured for over two months. This was Monty's first role coached by Mira Rostova. Critics did not like the show, probably because they were tired of watching plays that had war as the central subject, long dialogues and little action on stage. Nevertheless, Monty's interpretation was unanimously acclaimed. Robert Garland of the *New York Journal-American* wrote: "Montgomery Clift, recently of *The Searching Wind*, is as touching as he is terrifying in the role of the returned soldier."[56] Howard Barnes of the *New York Herald Tribune* added, "Montgomery Clift plays the part with superb authority."[57] While Burton Rascoe of the *New York World-Telegram* said: "*Foxhole in the Parlor* belongs on any well-chosen list of season's best.... The brilliant young actor Montgomery Clift has shown he can carry a whole play with the feeling and conviction he gave to a minor role in *The Searching Wind*."[58]

In order to catch more media attention, the theater's management paid a group of girls to wait for Monty outside the theater at the end of show. He was completely disinterested in this however, and he only wanted to act. He was a perfectionist who did not allow any noise when he was on stage. During the performance he ordered that all the air-conditioning be turned off because it would bother his concentration, and he paid no attention to the needs of the audience.

Actress Ann Lincoln, who was working with him in the play, fell madly in love with him. They would spend weekends together and they took a trip to Mexico, where they talked about a possible engagement. But, as with what previously happened with Phillis Thaxter, Ann did not take long to realize that things were not working as they should. Ann was a beautiful woman, but very insecure (later this insecurity would lead her to alcoholism) and she tried to make him jealous by having an affair with his brother Brooks and with Marlon Brando.

Monty got really angry with his brother, and during a strong argument heard that Brooks rescued Ann from committing suicide, caused by Monty's rejection. Lincoln always stayed in touch with Monty, and he often helped her with money when she asked. He even included her in his will and left her a little sum.

In a letter sent to Kevin McCarthy during the summer of 1945, Monty talks about his friendship with Thornton Wilder: "This is a real intellectual ... who can speak with infinite knowledge and above all Truth about that which most concerns me — The Theater and its allied arts."[59] Like Monty, Wilder had a twin sister and the actor would tell him how close he felt to her even after she went to college and then married a lawyer and moved to Austin, Texas.

Within a short time, the playwright became like a mentor to Monty and, as Isabel Wilder remembered, he often would ask him: "And now what should I do next?" He was beginning to be after parts in the movies and on stage, and he was not old enough to judge himself just what he could do or could not do, and there weren't many parts ready for him yet because he was still so young.

"Well Thornton was great about that. He knew the theater and parts so well and he could suggest plays and say perhaps you can do this."[60]

Monty and Thornton had a lot in common. They shared the same restless, reserved, lonely, well-traveled, romantic character, as well as the same sexual preferences.

After *The Skin of Our Teeth,* Wilder did not write any other plays. He started many projects, all of which were left uncompleted. One of those was a play called *The Emporium,* written exclusively with Monty in mind. It was the story of a young man who spent his life trying to work in a big, mysterious department store, whose manager always hired the most unqualified employees. Wilder worked on this project for over 10 years and he announced many times that he was ready to produce it with Monty as the protagonist. But, he was a perfectionist and he was always dissatisfied with the final result. He finally gave up, greatly disappointing the young actor. In the summer of 1945, even though Mira and Thornton did not agree with his choice, Monty went to Hollywood at Warner's invitation to screen test for *Pursuit*. It was a failure, and the part went to another young actor, Robert Mitchum, who was unknown at the time.

Even if his success on stage was extraordinary, Monty still could not get all the parts he wished for. When he heard that Guthrie McClintic, Katharine Cornell's husband, was preparing a production of George Bernard Shaw's *Candide,* he desperately tried to get the part of March Banks but McClintic chose Marlon Brando instead.

During that summer, the director gave him the role of Hadrian, in the romantic comedy *You Touched Me!* He was trying to decide whether to cast Monty or Phil Brown, so he asked the advice of author Tennessee Williams, who co-wrote the play with Donald Windham. Williams replied to him by wire: "'Practically a toss up. Clift has more experience and charm. Brown has more foxy upstart quality. I have dysentery. You decide.'"[61]

The play, based on a D.H. Lawrence short story, was about overcoming repression, sexual and otherwise. Monty played a Canadian pilot who falls in love with a shy English girl with the encouragement of the girl's father, a sea captain.

Monty was excited to work in a Tennessee Williams' play, especially since he had just had incredible success with *The Glass Menagerie.* Actor John Springer recalls that Monty one day told him: "'There is a show in Chicago, which is supposed to be going to New York, but it is simply dying at the box office. Claudia Cassidy, a critic here, is desperately trying to keep it alive, and all of us working in the theater are doing everything we can to get people excited about it. Will you come to see it tomorrow?' ... God knows how many times Monty had seen it, but throughout he was giggling, crying and grabbing my arm and whispering, 'Isn't it marvelous, just marvelous?' Afterwards we went back to Laurette Taylor's dressing room and Monty all of a sudden fell on his knee and started kissing the hem of her dressing gown, while she tried to shoo him off: 'Montgomery, you silly boy, stop that this minute!'"

Springer remembers that Monty often behaved strangely, like when they both went to an Ella Fitzgerald concert and he went up to her between songs, knelt before her and said, "You Goddess!"[62]

You Touched Me! earned mediocre reviews and suffered in the inevitable comparisons to *The Glass Menagerie,* but again Monty's performance was better received than the play.

During the three-month run of the show, Monty tried to experiment with different acting techniques, probably at the suggestion Mira Rostova,

Monty preparing his own coffee in a special coffee maker bought in Italy.

who used to spend hours in his dressing room discussing the performance. Monty tried to lower his tone of voice to give a better sense of romanticism and mystery to his character, Hadrian. In his opinion, this trick made the audience concentrate harder to hear his lines. In addition, he started to improvise different movements on stage, upsetting the rest of the cast.

Monty had the opportunity to get to know the two authors of the comedy. From the beginning, he did not like Williams that much, probably because of the writer's open homosexuality, which was completely different from his own. Williams remembered, "I was beguiled by his very feminine beauty. Monty was the loveliest man in the world then, and he was considered the finest young American actor.... I was mesmerized by his eyes. They were like a wounded bird's."[63]

On the other hand, Monty established a long friendship with Donald Windham which also included Windham's lifetime companion, actor Sandy Campbell. "Monty was perfect as Hadrian" recalls the writer; "often he would come to visit us and sometimes the three of us went to bed together."[64] But although there was some kind of physical intimacy, Monty was still very secretive about his sentimental and sexual life. Often Windham was invited for dinner at Monty's parents' house on Park Avenue. "It was an honor for me! His mother was really a terrible woman. After Monty died, she was still having dinner parties inviting all her son's friends trying to control everybody's life."[65]

You Touched Me! closed in January 1946. Three years later, Monty bought the screen rights, hoping to involve a Hollywood studio in producing the movie, but the script he wrote with Kevin McCarthy was, as Windham recalls, "Awful, full of vulgarities and trivialities."[66]

THREE

Hollywood

"Acting is a great form of art and a shitty profession!"
— *Montgomery Clift*

Although the screen test for Warner Bros. was a failure, Monty remained in high demand by other studios. MGM was openly courting him, but this did not help him in overcoming his caution: at the time, movie stars were considered vulgar celebrities not real artists as were theater actors.

During the Christmas holidays of 1946, Monty went skiing in Utah. In a postcard addressed to Donald Windham and Sandy Campbell, he wrote: "Hollywood is waving its fairy ugly finger at me,"[1] referring to the important offers that he was receiving daily. After his agent, Leland Haywarth, went to Hollywood to meet with MGM, Monty finally agreed to meet with Louis B. Mayer, who was ready to offer him an exclusive, six-month contract. During his two-month stay in Los Angeles, Monty wrote a lot of letters to his friends in New York. All of them were datelined with: "Vomit, California." "Hollywood is a terrible place and I shall want an explanation when I get back as to why the hell I'm here."[2]

After Monty participated in long screen tests to verify his photogenic qualities, Mayer offered him a seven-year extension of his contract. Monty wanted to be free. Personally taking care of his own decision, he left California in May 1946 at the end of his six-month trial contract, with his friends Jeanne and Fred Green. They traveled back home in his family's old car, which he had named "Beulah." It was a pleasant 14 day trip across the country. He stopped in New Orleans, where he went to have his amoebic dysentery checked by a specialist at the Tulane Medical Center.

Jeanne remembers: "It was hot and we were going into the French Quarter every night to eat…. He was alive and wonderful for five or six days. There was one night I remember very well that Monty said very quietly and gently — I'm going by myself — Fred was delighted because he was pleased to go to bed and I said: — Can I come? — No — he said — I wanna go by myself — and because he never wanted to hurt you, he just patted my face — I need to be alone — he said — Do you understand that? — I said I understood it. But I remember feeling like a child left behind, who has not been allowed to come playing. Looking back at that night, I recognized that probably it was something that I was to see a lot later on and not know what to make out of it."[3]

Once in New York, the Greens moved into Monty's new apartment on East 61st Street, which Jeanne helped to furnish. Strange people would come to the apartment at all hours, because Monty often invited strangers over after a night in a club. As Jeanne said: "Monty led many lives, we were only part of one of them."[4]

Actor Karl Malden and his wife Mona used to live right next door to Monty. When he wanted to see them, he used to walk up the fire escape, cross the roof and knock on their window instead of walking down three flights then up four. Malden recalls him always being very excited about acting and hungry for conversations about it. They became good friends and spent two Christmases at Monty's family's apartment on Park Avenue. "The holidays in the Clift house were like nothing I had ever seen before," Karl Malden wrote. "An enormous tree exquisitely decorated, Czech silver, beaded ornament. All very uptown. Everything perfect."

"Monty's mother was in the habit to invite her son's close friends to check up on him. I remember once she invited Mona. Mona was terrified of this elegant lady, but she went ahead and met her at some classy hotel. When Mona returned home she burst into tears. Through her sobbing, she managed to explain that Mrs. Clift had talked about 'the Jews' all throughout the meal, never realizing she was sitting across from Mona Greenberg. Mona became hysterical not so much because of what Mrs. Clift had said, but because she was so furious with herself for not saying anything in response."[5]

Bobby Lewis wanted Monty for the role of Treplev in Chekov's *The Seagull*. In order to convince him, he told him that the very first production of the play had the great Meyerhold, a famous rebellious theater artist, as the protagonist, Treplev, at the Moscow Art Theatre. Monty firmly refused the part because he was tired of always playing the "sensitive man." He was trying to escape from the image that Broadway had created for him. Instead, he was very attracted to the idea of playing a cowboy next to John Wayne in *Red River,* directed by Howard Hawks.

The director was already a Hollywood "veteran," and at the time he had made more than 30 films. Many of these films were big hits, and he discovered actresses like Carol Lombard and Lauren Bacall. Hawks had been impressed by Monty's performance in *You Touched Me!* (he had met with him backstage on one of the last days that the show was running), but he made his final decision only after a meeting with Clift's agent, Leland Hayward. At that time, Hayward was having an affair with Hawks' wife, Keith Slim.

It was actually Slim who convinced her husband to pick Monty for the part. The problem, though, was Monty's indecision; remembering his first bad screen test experience, he did not feel

Monty talking in the street with an unidentified friend. He is wearing his favorite outfit: white button-down shirt, khaki pants, checked socks and penny-loafers, 1949.

ready for Hollywood. Friends like Mira Rostova and Bobby Lewis strongly advised him not to accept it. Only Lehman Engel thought it was absolutely crazy to refuse an offer made by somebody as important as Hawks.

On his part, Hayward was anxious to close the deal. He called Keith and asked her to invite both him and Monty for lunch.

Slim remembered this in her autobiography:

> It was very clear from the minute Clift walked in that he wasn't at all interested in making an "oater." He was, it appeared, even less interested in Howard Hawks. What did catch his eyes was me…. After lunch, Leland and Howard began to negotiate a deal, on the off chance that Monty might agree to do the film…. I took Monty by the arm, and suggested we have a walk in the garden. Howard nodded, Leland grinned. As soon as we were out of earshot, Monty asked me: — Should I do this? — Absolutely — But it is a Western — Howard can make a great Western — The thing is— Clift said — I do not know how to ride a horse or shoot a gun or walk in funny

boots—Well, that's the easy part. You learn all that very quickly. More importantly, what you will learn from Howard Hawks will be invaluable for the rest of your motion picture career, provided you intend to have one. You'll have two first-rate teachers—John Wayne who understands his craft and is a generous, nice man, and Howard, who's as good as they get—

Those lovely questioning gray eyes looked into mine, and then he said—"Okay I will—"

Into the house we went. Howard and Leland looked up in surprise—we were back too soon. Monty announced—"I've decided to do it. She talked me into it—"

Howard was amazed, I was amazed and Leland was ecstatic.[6]

Hayward obtained a $50,000 deal, with paid expenses and bonuses added throughout the shooting. He ended up with a total of $75,000, almost the same amount that was paid to Wayne. This was an extraordinary salary for someone's first appearance on the big screen.

Hawks immediately took care of his new "discovery" by challenging Monty to learn how to ride like a real cowboy: "Now look, this is a Western, if you can't sit on a horse, you may as well go right home."[7] Monty was trained by Richard Farnsworth, a famous stuntman and Monty's body double in the movie. Farnsworth taught him all the tricks that he needed to know to play the part of a believable cowboy.

Quickly Monty learned how to roll a cigarette, how to fight without hurting someone else or without being hurt himself, and how to rapidly draw out a pistol. Hawks realized that Monty was working very hard. In just three weeks he was not only able to use a gun well, but to also ride horses like a professional cowboy.[8]

Red River was based on a story called *The Chisholm Trail,* written by Borden Chase. The original title was

Between takes for *Red River* on location in Tucson, Arizona.

Monty with John Wayne on the set of **Red River**, 1946.

The River Is Red as taken from a part of the dialogue which was later cut during the editing process. In this, a reference was made to Indian blood coloring the waters of the river. Monty played Matthew Garth, the adopted son of John Wayne's character, Tom Dunson. Matthew lost his parents during the same Indian attack in which Dunson's girlfriend was killed. Eighteen years later, the two cowboys plan to drive cattle from Texas to Mission along the Chisholm Trail which crosses the Red River. During the drive, Matthew tries to rebel against Tom's tyrannical authority. Dunson has become a very cruel and ruthless man, and the two cowboys have a head-on confrontation in which Monty disarms and leaves Wayne to his own destiny.

Hawks superbly showed the huge physical and psychological differences between the two characters: Monty's height was 5' 10" and Wayne's height was 6' 4". He contrasted Matthew Garth's almost feminine sensitivity with Tom's macho behavior.

It took 14 days of shooting to complete the final fighting scene. It was a very difficult and key frame, especially because Monty had to pit himself against Wayne who was already considered an icon in the Western genre. At the beginning of the shooting, Wayne laughed off his colleague's clumsy attempts to punch him correctly, but he soon changed his mind. Monty had trained himself so well that he perfectly matched Wayne's toughness. The final showdown represents the climax of *Red River* and it is a symbol of the clash between two different monumental forces.

Monty was very excited to follow Hawks' direction. Hawks wanted him to portray Matthew's character perfectly, especially focusing on little details such as the way he walked and moved, while leaving part of it for Monty to improvise. Monty loved to improvise and attained excellent results in standing up to the majestic and authoritative presence of Wayne. Never again will there be a Western cowboy who appeared more sophisticated and graceful than Monty.

The making of *Red River* lasted until the end of December, for a total of five months. Monty did not socialize with other cast members. At the beginning he tried to behave "normally" by going bear hunting with John Wayne and David Hawks, the director's son, or by playing poker with the other actors. As he would later confess to his friend Ben Bagley: "They laughed and drank and told dirty jokes and slapped each other on the back. They tried to draw … me into their circle but I couldn't go along with them. The machismo thing repelled me because it seemed so forced and unnecessary."[9]

Actors Walter Brennan and John Ireland were the only ones with whom Monty liked to spend free time or rehearse his lines. Hawks was not very fond of Ireland, because he was having an affair with actress Joanne Dru, a woman who was also an object of the director's attention. Ireland also angered Hawks by drinking too much and by often being late. The director took his revenge during the editing process by further reducing the part of Cherry Valance, who was played by Ireland. Nevertheless, Dru and Ireland were married soon after the movie was completed.

Shelley Winters was one of the extras in the film. The young actress had already seen Monty on the Broadway stage and she admired him tremendously. She is only visible in a short close up next to Monty, because the longer scene in which she invited him dancing ended up on the cutting room floor. Winters remembers: "He was very shy and spoke in a mumble and sort of reminded me of an early Jimmy Stewart. But Monty was beautiful and radiated a kind of spiritual and physical graciousness. He took my hand, looked into my eyes and said: 'How are you?' and I answered 'I'm okay now….' Before he let go my hand, he said in a husky voice, 'I hope we really work together sometime.' 'I hope so, too,' I replied."[10] Later they would work together again in George Stevens' *A Place in the Sun*.

Monty often went to visit the Greens in Palm Springs during one of the several cancellations that the shooting had due to heavy rain. *Red River* was, in fact, shot almost completely on location in the Rain Valley of Arizona, near the Mexican border. In Palm Springs, Monty helped the Greens build their new house or sometimes he would invite them to stay with him in his Beverly Hills suite. According to Fred Green, Monty had an affair at the time with the wife of a West Hollywood dentist.[11] He would disappear for hours without notification. When *Red River* was finally completed, Monty visited his twin sister and her husband in Austin, Texas, before traveling to New Orleans for his regular check up on his amoebic dysentery.

A publicity still as the cowboy Matthew Garth in Howart Hawks' *Red River.*

He loved New Orleans, with its atmosphere, and the clubs in which he could listen to the best jazz. But one night, he lost control in a bar after drinking heavily. Monty started screaming wildly, rolling on the floor and annoying the audience. He ended up in a police station where he spent the night in jail, accused of vagrancy. In a letter to the Greens, he wrote that it turned out to be quite a happy situation. He shared a cell with drunks who sang, danced and smoked all night. There was a young drag queen among the inmates, who performed a funny, much applauded striptease. Finally, the judge released him the next morning.

The bad weather made it impossible to stick to the budget or to the timing scheduled for the making of the film. It cost over $3 million to make, more than double what was expected. It was a very delicate situation since the movie was produced by the director himself, in order to be free of any constraints from Hollywood studios. This Monterey Production project, which was the name of Hawks' production studio, risked sinking even before the film was completed. Hawks also encountered many difficulties while editing the movie, whose release was postponed several times. At that time, film editing and distribution normally did not take more than six months. In this case, due to a legal litigation with co-producer tycoon Howard Hughes, it took over a year and a half.

When Monty attended a rough-cut of *Red River,* he thought that the film was mediocre. He wrote in a letter to Kevin McCarthy that he was ashamed of himself, but in a letter to writer James Jones, he was convinced that the movie would be a commercial hit and would make him into a star: "I knew that I was going to be famous so I decided I would get drunk anonymously one last time."[12]

As Monty predicted, *Red River* had enormous success at the box office, earning about 4 million dollars and reaching the Variety list as the third most seen movie in 1948.[13] Critics were enthusiastic, although many did not like the happy ending that Hawks added to Borden Chase's original screenplay. The author thought the movie was "garbage."[14] The *New York Times* called *Red River* "one of the best cowboy pictures ever made … for at least two thirds of the way."[15]

Although he told everybody that he wanted to take a period of rest as soon as the shooting was completed, Monty accepted the invitation of screenwriter Peter Viertel, Salka Viertel's son, to meet with Austrian director Fred Zinnemann, who had planned to make a movie with him in mind. As Zinnemann recalled in his autobiography: "It was immediately clear that Monty was the right choice: exuberant and full of energy, he was an electrifying personality. Most important there was no danger of our picture becoming the vehicle for a star, as he was quite unknown to the general public, having only finished his first film.

"Clift asked if he could see the script. I told him there was nothing on paper, but that a Swiss writer Richard Schweizer, had started to work on a screenplay. As soon as you have something, let me know and I will come over."[16]

Three months later, upon his return to New York in May 1947, Monty received a 15-page outline of the script from Swiss producer Lazar Wechsler.[17] The following August he received a complete script titled *The European Children*, which was later changed into *The Search*. It was based on an article about war orphans.[18]

Forty-year-old Fred Zinnemann had emigrated to the United States eighteen years before. At the beginning he worked as an extra, and then he directed some short documentaries, followed by a long motion picture. In 1944, *The Seventh Cross* starring Spencer Tracy and produced by MGM was his first success.

The Search was inspired by real events, and was shot in a semidocumentary style with a crew of 10 people in a studio in Zurich, Switzerland. It was also shot in some German locations that had been hit by the war, something quite exceptional for a time when all films were usually shot in studio interiors. Monty played Ralph, a G.I., who finds a little refugee boy in a German town destroyed by bombs. After trying to locate his parents, he decides to take him with him to America. The child, who at the beginning is very hostile and refuses to speak, gradually attaches himself to the soldier until destiny reunites him with his mother.

After several arguments with Zinnemann, Peter Viertel quit, because either the director or the producer, Wechsler, insisted on removing every possible direct allusion to the Nazis. The terrible situation of displaced children would be treated as a humanitarian problem, not as a tragic consequence of a German attack. In fact, in the movie the words Nazi and Hitler are never mentioned. Zinnemann explained: "It was most important to make the innocent American audience aware of what had happened in Europe, for this reason we were obliged to soften the truth. Otherwise people would have been unable to bear it…. And we did want as many Americans as possible to see it."[19]

Monty did not like the softer script. As Viertel, he believed that the audience should have been reminded of the Nazis' genocide. Monty accepted the part and signed a $75,000 contract which included the possibility of changing his character's lines and of being able to quit at any moment, without any financial penalty as long as six weeks had passed from the beginning of the film.

In May 1947, Monty arrived at the Hotel Storchen in Zurich, where Fred Zinnemann and his wife Renée were staying: "Hi I'm Monty, I'm starving…. Let's eat."[20] That was the way in which he introduced himself to Mrs. Zinnemann in the lobby of the hotel as soon as he arrived. "There seemed to be no moment of strangeness between us: it was as if I had known him all my life."[21]

The big surprise was that he arrived with Mira Rostova who would serve as his personal coach. During the making of *The Search*, Monty often disappeared with her in his room to work on the screenplay. To prepare himself for this part, Monty moved into an army engineers' unit outside Zurich for a while, in order to observe the routine of military life and the behavior of soldiers. While there, he was invited to a special screening of a German documentary on concentration camps. The scenes of the masses of Jews being deported and gassed, and seeing their bodies piled up in trenches made him sick, and he was unable to sit through the whole film. He suddenly left the screening room to vomit outside.

Monty found his part to be too sentimental and he was very dissatisfied with his lines, so he decided to rewrite his part with Mira's help. He wanted to make his character more "real" without being the typical stereotype of an American soldier. Zinnemann appreciated a lot of these changes, and felt that they saved the movie from being a disaster.[22]

The part of the little refugee was magnificently played by Ivan Jandl. He was discovered while Zinnemann was in Prague to meet with famous Czech soprano Jarmila Novotna, who played the part of the mother. Jandl was only ten years old, but his voice was very well known on the Czech radio. Although the child only spoke Czech, he quickly memorized all his lines, and was helped along by Monty's friendship and affection.

Monty used to bring him little presents and go for long walks in his company, always treating him like an adult. Looking at photographs taken on the set, it is easy to recognize Monty's love for children, a "passion" that he also displayed for little Timi Zinnemann, and above all for Flip, the McCarthys' son. In a beautiful reportage by *Movie Life* magazine, Monty was photographed while playing with Jandl, and he almost looks as if he, himself, is a child.[23] On the set of *The Search,* the only reasons for disagreement with the director were related to Mira Rostova's constant presence near the camera, from which she used to give her approval or disapproval of Monty's acting with a slight nod or shake of her head. For many weeks Zinnemann did not say a word about it, but he eventually managed to make her leave. His action, though, did not stop her from continuing to coach Monty off the set. In later years, Mira's presence would also bother directors such as George Stevens, Alfred Hitchcock and Elia Kazan.

Monty's friendship with the Zinnemanns became stronger after a day of happy sailing with Renée and Timi on Lake Zurich. When the boat reached the middle of the lake, Monty decided to take a dip. After jumping over the side, the force of the dive, combined with a gust of wind and the strong current, moved the boat away from him. Monty knew that Timi could not swim, but screamed to Renée to hang him onto a rope so that he would become a sort of human anchor. This slowed the boat down and Monty was able to reach them and take back the helm. He became a hero, and the idea of having accomplished an act of manly behavior made him happy.

Because of some problems with the script and continuous interference from the producer, the making of *The Search* was not a completely happy experience for Monty, as showed in a letter written to his friend Ned Smith dated October 17, 1947: "Smythe — old man — I would like to write you of other things than the disgusting work I just finished. Unfortunately to work + have time off in the evenings or Sundays was not to be this time."[24]

Besides those complaints, Monty was content with the final result of the film (certainly more than *Red River*), which received an Academy Award for best screenplay. He was also nominated for best actor, but the Oscar went to Laurence Olivier for *Hamlet*. Monty was not disappointed because he was aware of the importance of already having received a nomination with his film debut and winning over Olivier would have been too much. Ivan Jandl won a special Oscar for young actors. Zinnemann comments on him in his autobiography in 1992: "Ivan, now in his forties, lives in Prague and is going bald, or so I thought, until I heard that he had died — alone and forgotten a year ago. It seems that the Oscar he received had brought him nothing but bad luck. The regime punished him for getting a splendid award from the 'capitalist West'; they did not allow him to work in films and forbade him to accept foreign contracts or to travel abroad."[25]

The Search opened in March 1948, a few months before *Red River* and for this reason it is considered Monty's first appearance on the screen. It was not a commercial success because of its limited distribution. One of the greatest compliments Monty ever received once the film was first shown in America, was when someone asked Zinnemann, "Where did you find a soldier who could act so well?" It was an ideal tribute to the authenticity of Monty's portrayal.[26]

In September 1948, when *Red River* opened in the theaters, Monty was invited to a couple of radio programs where he also talked about *The Search*. During the broadcast, he revealed that the children used in the movie were actual refugees, and that little Ivan Jandl had some health problems while making the film. It is possible to see this in the scene in which Jandl escapes from the orphanage and he is barely able to walk. Monty also talked in a mocking tone about the role of being a so-called rising movie star and about all the fuss that magazines made about his performance and his beauty, such as: "All the girls in eighth grade fell in love with Montgomery Clift."[27]

Back in New York, Monty started a frantic pace of life: he worked out daily at Stillman's gym, took singing lessons and bought as many books as he could read, piling them up in his apartment. Books were always his passion. He would spend a lot of time in old bookstores like Brentano's or Gotham, sitting on the floor and looking through boxes full of volumes in the back of the shop for books about theater history and stage designing. His personal library was filled not only with classics like Chekhov and Shakespeare, but also with the latest best sellers.

On October 5, 1945, Monty attended an acting class held at the Actors Studio, a new theatrical group created by Elia Kazan, Bobby Lewis and Cheryl Crawford. Lessons were taught in the crummy rooms of Malin Studios on 47th Street, not far from Broadway. Shortly thereafter, that location would become "the place" to learn and study acting and where new actors would go to be discovered. Only professional actors were admitted to the classes, and only after they passed a long series of interviews and auditions. "It is not a school," Kazan used to say. "Actors can come and actors can go."[28] The concept also included directors and authors, all of whom were united by the same desire to bravely practice their own craft in a way that was very different from commercial methods.

Kazan taught the beginners' class and Lewis was in charge of the advanced workshop. Among the 52 names on his roster were: Marlon Brando, Eli Wallach, Maureen Stapleton, Karl Malden, Kevin McCarthy and Montgomery Clift.

Crawford's contribution to the studio was strictly that of an administrator. After only one year, Robert Lewis walked out after a quarrel with Kazan. The young director, along with Lee Strasberg, renewed the spirit of the Actors Studio by introducing the "Method," an absolutely new style of acting free of any mannerisms or rules.

The Method was an adaptation of an acting technique created by Konstantin Stanislavski at the beginning of the last century, and used by the Moscow Art Theatre's company. It was based on psychological realism with complete identification between actor and character. Preparation included so-called "private moments." One of the more intense elements of the technique, in which actors had to sing, strip or play with themselves, involved talking about their own personal experiences, including those that were the most painful. Actors were all using complete freedom of expression in order to reach a state of total personal awareness that they could then apply to their acting. All characters had to have their own interior lives and could not be just a stereotype, such as the mere personification of good or evil.

Lee Strasberg assigned Monty and Maureen Stapleton a scene from Dostoevsky's *Crime and Punishment*. The two spent long days rehearsing in Stapleton's apartment, trying to apply everything they had learned in class. Monty also spent many hours with Marlon Brando, talking about their parts. They appeared together in amateurish film footage shot by Kevin McCarthy, in which they imitated characters from the silent comedies of the 1920's, something that Monty often used to do for his friends.

Monty hoped that this experimental acting school would allow him the opportunity to confront new roles that were very different from the ones he had interpreted so far. He wanted to test his talent without being stuck with the usual parts. But Strasberg and the other teachers kept proposing conventional roles for him, like Shakespeare's *Romeo and Juliet* of which Monty tried to give an original interpretation. He also asked for advice on how to play a modern Romeo from his close friend Jerome Robbins, who would later become one of the most famous choreographers on Broadway. This would inspire Robbins with the idea for his production of *West Side Story*.

But after a couple of disappointing months, Monty left the Actors Studio. Using his own intelligence and imagination, he studied new characters by himself, paying attention to their psychology, their way of speaking and gesturing, as well as their most significant physical characteristics. As Arthur Miller recalls, Monty thought of Lee Strasberg as a "charlatan."[29] According to Mira Rostova, none of Monty's interpretations during his career were close to his real personality.[30] When in 1959 in an interview he was asked if he was a "Method" actor, Monty replied, "I wish I knew what that means. Me. I just act."[31]

All of a sudden, Monty's career was booming. Alfred Hitchcock approached him with *Rope*, the story of a murder committed by a young, high-society gay couple in New York against a friend. Monty would have played the part that James Stewart eventually got. The subject was very delicate and the play had already been the object of a big controversy, in part for the explicit homosexuality of its characters. Monty, who lived in fear of having his sexuality exposed, turned down the offer.

In June 1948, he began shooting *The Heiress*, with Olivia de Havilland, in Hollywood. She proposed to director William Wyler the idea of making a movie from Henry James' popular novel *Washington Square*. Monty accepted the part of Morris Townsend because it gave him the opportunity to act as a character with an interesting personality, not just playing "the good" character as he did in his previous two films. In his first meeting with screenwriters Ruth and Augustus Goetz, Monty awakened some confusion by showing up wearing a tattered jacket, a pair of jeans and a T-shirt. Augustus Goetz said, "He looked like a bum and I thought how can he ever play the suave elegant Townsend? But once he wore the beautiful costumes made by Edith Head suddenly he seemed perfect for that part."[32]

Making *The Heiress* was not a happy experience because the set was rife with rivalry and antagonism. Monty was annoyed with British stage actor Ralph Richardson, who was making his first American film. He was cast in the role of the father and acted in a very theatrical manner as if he was still on stage.

Furthermore, Olivia de Havilland would often arrive without having memorized her lines, demanding Wyler direct her in front of the camera in every little movement and detail. On the other hand, the actress accused Monty of thinking only about himself in each of the scenes they had together. She felt that he was too stubborn and precise about his own

With Olivia de Havilland in *The Heiress*, 1949.

acting, and hated the fact that he insisted on singing and playing the piano, himself, during a love scene with her.

Monty was also convinced that William Wyler was too cold in his manner of directing, and that he favored his female star. The truth was that the director had accepted Olivia de Havilland due to pressure by Paramount, but they did not get along. She thought Wyler was a bully and a tyrant who demanded too many takes, while the director thought de Havilland was not willing to look as dull as the role of Catherine required. Eventually, they communicated only through an assistant director.

Again Mira Rostova created a few problems by being on the set, especially to de Havilland, who complained that she had to act in front of an actor who was always looking in the opposite direction: at Rostova and not at her. During this period Monty came closer to living the Hollywood high life than any other time. He spent many nights in the company of the Greens and often spent weekends playing tennis with Charlie Chaplin at William Wyler's mansion above the Beverly Hills Hotel.

Occasionally, Chaplin took him to dinner at Salka Viertel's, which was a gathering place for many European intellectuals like Thomas Mann, Bertholt Brecht and Aldous Huxley. Monty felt a great sense of admiration for Viertel's courage and for her *"joie de vivre."* She would be the one to introduce him to Greta Garbo, with whom she was rumored to have been a lover. When Garbo retired in her golden, solitary New York apartment, she often visited Monty at his townhouse on 61st Street. They shared a total contempt for Hollywood.

Shelley Winters remembers an episode that happened in those days at a party given by Gene Kelly. "I noticed in a dark convertible two people necking in a rather sexual manner. When I peeked again, I realized it was Montgomery Clift and Salka Viertel, Garbo's writer and a very important person in Hollywood firmament. She was also about sixty

Monty as fortune hunter Morris Townsend in *The Heiress,* 1949.

years old…. I wonder wistfully if Aidan Quinn perhaps likes necking with sixty year old ladies."[33]

Monty started to drink heavily during that time. Some guests at Viertel's swore they saw him drunk and walking on all fours or kneeling before his host. Billy LeMassena noticed that since his friend moved to Hollywood, drinking had become a serious problem, and Monty would often turn against his parents in fits of rage. "The Clifts were broken-hearted. They could not understand it, none of us could, or what had suddenly caused it. Looking back, I think he had found a total denial of the life he once knew. I think it is a cop out to blame his mother's influence in his upbringing. No, it was a whole reversal of behavior. His had been a life of coded behavior, impeccable manners, politeness, clean living, and when he got to Hollywood he found the people high up couldn't be trusted. He could no longer take people at their face value and that's what set him off…. He was turned by Hollywood, no question about that. There was an evil that confronted him and he could not handle it."[34]

The American audience was impressed by the end of *The Heiress,* in which Olivia de Havilland leaves Monty banging on her door (built bigger

Monty and Olivia de Havilland in a publicity still from *The Heiress*, 1949.

on purpose to draw attention to Monty's ineffective knocking). Usually Hollywood stereotypes ensured that the leading male character was never refused, as he was in this case, but always eventually won back the girl.

Paramount asked Monty to attend the Hollywood premiere of *The Heiress* at the Grauman Chinese Theatre in the company of 17-year-old actress Elizabeth Taylor, who had been chosen to be his co-star in his next movie *A Place in the Sun*. Monty tried to give every excuse not to go because he disliked attending all types of public events, especially with unknown, young starlets.

But when beautiful and elegant Elizabeth Taylor appeared on his doorstep, he was incapable of turning her down. Therefore, they arrived together at the theater in a limousine, where they were greeted by a group of fans and photographers, all of whom were mesmerized by their glamour. The flashes of the cameras went crazy when Elizabeth stopped for a moment to fix Monty's bow tie before going into the theater. That photograph was published in magazines worldwide. During the showing of the movie, Elizabeth noticed Monty slipping down under the chair, embarrassed by his acting which he thought was very bad. On their way out, Monty called Elizabeth "Bessie Mae," a nickname which was to be his private name for her from then on.

Previously, Elizabeth had met Monty in director George Stevens' office when they discussed *A Place in the Sun* but he probably had not even noticed her. "I had the full scale of teenage palpitations. I thought he was the most gorgeous thing in the world and easily one of the best actors. But in a pair of jeans, slouched in a chair, he was hardly the austere, mysterious, affected Method Studio actor I was expecting. And he wasn't a bit snide about acting with a 'cheap movie star.'"[35]

The Heiress was praised by critics and Olivia de Havilland won an Academy Award for best actress.

In October, before resuming work, Monty took a long trip to Europe and to the Middle East. London was his first stop, where he went to see Laurence Olivier acting at the Old Vic and had dinner with him. Then he crossed the channel by boat to reach Paris, where he visited the Louvre and spent a night at the Opéra and at La Comédie Française. One day Alice Toklas invited him, along with Thornton and Isabel Wilder, for tea at the home of Gertrude Stein, her lifetime companion. There, Monty admired Stein's personal collection of rare Picassos, Matisses and Cézannes.

In a letter to Donald Windham, Stein wrote: "Alice had met Monty when Thornton brought him to Rue de Christine in 1948. She remembers him distinctly; however her impression of him was different from ours, 'a well-mannered but dull boy. He uses his charm the way a woman does, not a man.'"[36]

Fixing make-up, between takes in Lake Tahoe, Nevada, on the set of *A Place in the Sun.*

A few years later, Toklas' impression was not changed. Monty and Libby Holman knocked on her door saying they were on their way to Tangier to see Paul and Jane Bowles. They wanted to know if she had a message that they should take to them from her.

His beloved Rome was the third destination of Monty's trip. "Rome is a city of hills and walls and hills," he used to say. He loved the fountains, the small streets and the unique color of the sky "pink over pink." He particularly liked the Campidoglio with its endless, beautiful stairs.[37] He spent Thanksgiving there and he loved Italian expresso, buying a special coffee maker to bring back to New York with him.

The journey continued to Athens and on to Jerusalem, where he met Zinnemann, who was interested in making a documentary-style film like *The Search,* but set in the sacred location. Monty seemed interested in the project, and traveled with the director to the Dead Sea. Later they visited a kibbutz, which was suddenly attacked by a group of Arab warriors and Monty again became ill with amoebic dysentery. But overall it was an extraordinary experience that brought him closer to the Jewish people and strengthened his good feelings for them. This would help him to better understand his character when he acted as Noah Ackerman in *The Young Lions* and as Sigmund Freud in John Houston's *Freud.*

Monty with seventeen-year-old Elizabeth Taylor in a publicity shot for *A Place in the Sun,* 1949.

On the way back, Monty stopped in Cyprus. From there he flew to Switzerland, where he spent Christmas with Thornton and Isabel Wilder. In St. Moritz he received the news that he was on the cover of *Life* magazine and the focus of the article was on "New Male Movie Stars."[38]

It seems ironic that at the same time that Monty was becoming a popular sex symbol, rumors about people seeing him in bathhouses or gay bars began to spread. His lawyer avoided a scandal when he was arrested for trying to pick up a young boy on 42nd Street. The attorney hid the incident from the press; however, the gossip quickly reached the Hollywood industry. For his part, Monty did not understand the connection between his acting career and the sex appeal he held for women. He constantly complained to his friends about fans waiting for him outside his doorstep. "I have no time. No time!" was his answer to the journalists who continuously asked him about his love life.

Mira Rostova or starlets hand picked by the studio, escorted him to all the social events. The truth was that Monty was going out with Jerome Robbins, with whom he later broke up, as Brooks Clift maintained, when the choreographer reported a list of names of people in the entertainment business to the House Un–American Activities Committee.

It was at that time that the United States began an anti–Communist crusade, initiated by Senator Joseph McCarthy, whose purpose was to stop all presumed American Communist movements to subvert the State. A special committee was appointed to investigate the activities of unions or organizations, whose members belonged to the American Communist party. Many on the "black list" were filmmakers, whose only goals, according to McCarthy, were to spread socialist messages in their works— the so called "Red Tide." A list of ten filmmakers who refused to answer questions were identified, indicted and forced to appear in court. Being on the "black list" meant the end of the careers of many actors and directors, such as John Garfield.

Director Edward Dmytryk was among the ten, and was one of the few whose careers did not sink; in fact, he would direct Monty in two of his movies. Elia Kazan was also questioned for his left-wing sympathies and pressured to name some of

Monty at ease in his two-room walk-up apartment, 1949.

his colleagues. His confessions strangely did not jeopardize his friendship with Monty, who would work with him again in 1959 in *Wild River*.

Directors such as John Huston, William Wyler and others, along with actors like Humphrey Bogart, Lauren Bacall, Danny Kaye and Gene Kelly, organized a group to defend freedom of speech, marching and protesting in Washington, D.C. Monty did not get involved in the protest, but was always by the side of his friends who took part in it.

In spring 1949, Paramount invited Monty to come to Hollywood to discuss the possibility of being the protagonist in two films. The first one was *Sunset Boulevard,* directed by Billy Wilder and already in pre-production with legendary silent screen diva Gloria Swanson, who was cast as the leading female star. The second film was *An American Tragedy* (later renamed as *A Place in the Sun*), an adaptation of Theodore Dreiser's novel, starring Elizabeth Taylor. Monty was interested in the projects, but as with other movies that he was being considered for at the same time like *High Noon* and *The Naked and the Dead,* he did not rush to make any decisions.

The reason for his hesitation, which cost him parts in important films, was Libby Holman, who again showed up in his life seven years after *Mexican Mural*. Monty would spend all of his free time in Treetops, Connecticut, at Holman's country estate. They started a very mutually dependent relationship, based on alcohol, drug abuse and, perhaps, on sexual intimacy.

David Holman, Libby's nephew, stated in an interview to *Blueboy* magazine that, although he was very young, he had a crush on Monty and he slept with him, but he ruled out that his aunt did the same. "Monty was so drugged and drunk all the time. I never saw him when he wasn't drunk. Morning, noon or night…. We had a room next to one another at my Aunt Libby's. I found it unsatisfying. He just needed someone to hold and hit. He was passive in a way. He never had an erection. My Aunt Libby would kick him out of the bedroom. She prevented him from doing great, good movies…. He didn't understand how close they were; how dependent upon her he was. Jealous of his fame, she prevented him from doing good movies. And he listened to her and they would talk ten times a day on the phone, when he wasn't at the house. She'd read the scripts for him and say, 'You do not want to do this crap!' … One thing for sure, my aunt wasn't good for him. She was too influential for her own motives. She wanted control over him. Like she wanted over everybody. She would have known those terrific scripts would have been great for his career, instead she made him turn them down. Jealousy. She was jealous of his fame."[39]

Perhaps the rumors about his intimate friendship with Libby convinced Monty to turn down *Sunset Boulevard*. The plot was too similar to their real life story: a relationship between an old rich woman and a young screenwriter set in the golden but ambiguous Hollywood world.

Between spring and summer 1949, Monty moved into a small, $45 a month apartment on East 55th Street. In July, a young photographer named Stanley Kubrick would take photographs of Monty there for *Look* magazine. In the spread Monty appears lying on his bed close to a window, yawning, reading a script or sipping a cup of coffee.[40]

During this period of time he hired Arline Cunningham as his personal assistant. The girl was Monty's fan and came to New York just to meet her idol. Monty got to know her well and highly respected her judgment, so he shortly offered her a job. The position consisted of doing a selection of scripts, passing him only the ones that she thought were suitable for him to read. He would also take her with him to screenings and to the theater. She even went with him once to Germantown to visit the Foggs, his mother's adoptive parents. Arline fell madly in love with him,

Monty reading in his apartment a copy of Joseph Mitchell's **Old Mr. Flood,** 1949.

but for the next five years, they would only work together; their relationship was strictly professional, based solely on mutual esteem.

On the other hand, Monty's friendship with Mira was slowly transforming almost into a symbiosis; she became, as he would say, "my artistic conscience." She believed that Monty was totally split sexually and that
"this was the core of his tragedy, since he never stopped feeling guilty about
being conflicted."[41]

Donald Windham gives a different explanation for Monty's conflicts,
and for his future, self-destructive behavior, which made it impossible for
him to find excellent scripts that satisfied him.[42] (Monty would turn down
terrific screenplays of movies like *On the Waterfront* and *East of Eden.*) In
August 1949, Monty went back to Germany to make *The Big Lift,* a low
budget film produced by 20th Century–Fox. On his way to Berlin, he
stopped in London for a couple of weeks to visit the McCarthys, who were
living there in a small apartment in the heart of Chelsea. Kevin was, in
fact, playing in Arthur Miller's *Death of a Salesman* and Monty attended
a performance of the play. For a long time Monty and Kevin had been

discussing the idea of opening their own production company so they could choose only the work in which they were interested, but the idea was always postponed.

Upon his arrival in the German capital, Monty prepared for his role by just wandering in the streets between the ruins and the debris of the recent Allied bombing. He observed Germans spending hours in lines to get supplies and food. It was a very moving scene for a young, American actor.

Director George Seaton, who won an Academy Award in 1947 for *Miracle on 34th Street,* wrote the dialogue for *The Big Lift.* Monty liked the script, and he especially liked his lines. He considered them exceptional because comedic elements were blended with some realistic and suspenseful scenes. In fact, real soldiers were used as extras and original footage from newsreels was inserted in the film. *The Big Lift* was set in Berlin, which was divided into different sectors after the war. Monty was a naïve idealistic American sergeant, whose duty it was to bring food and supplies into the city sector that was not occupied by Soviets. During the story, he falls in love with a German girl who just uses him for her own personal advantage, as a friend, actor Paul Douglas, would discover.

As usual, Mira was near Monty at all times, generating so much tension that Seaton finally requested that she leave the set. Monty made it known that if Mira left, he, too, would leave. The director, therefore, had no choice but to let her stay. As a reporter on the set later recalled, Seaton was constantly contradicted by this little Russian lady, and he could not take it anymore. The atmosphere during the making of the movie became even more uncomfortable due to the rivalry between Paul Douglas and Monty during close-ups.

Although *The Big Lift* was a flop at the box office, it is the only movie where Monty shows his sense of humor, revealing a new and very different aspect of his acting career. *A Place in the Sun* was Monty's next project, to which he was committed between fall and winter 1949.

Director George Stevens asked the screenwriters to adapt the script as closely as possible to the original Theodore Dreiser novel. But Paramount wanted a romantic movie containing characters with whom audiences could easily identify. For a time the film title was *The Lovers,* but it was later changed to the one which was actually used. Due to the director's habit of shooting a huge amount of footage only to meticulously edit it down, the movie was not distributed in theaters until a year and half later.

Monty played the ambitious George Eastman, who kills his co-worker and his girlfriend, who was pregnant with his baby, in order to win the heart of a young and beautiful socialite. To prepare himself for the role,

Monty spent one night in the "death house" of California's San Quentin prison. Outdoor scenes were filmed in Lake Tahoe, Nevada, in complete isolation. Often, Stevens had the film's soundtrack playing between takes, the way it would later appear in the movie. At times, he also had the actors rehearse a scene without dialogue in order to test the intensity of the emotions with facial expressions or with head movements. Monty found Stevens' directions to be as rigid and inflexible as William Wyler's. He felt Stevens stuck with his own ideas and was not open to any suggestions or comments.

On this set Mira was also at Monty's side. Shelley Winters recalls: "She was his coach, nutritionist, friend and perhaps lover. And although she was on that film for the whole six months, Stevens never acknowledged her existence. He never said good morning to her or looked at her. Sometimes she would accidentally get her hand in front of the camera as she gave instructions to Monty, of course ruining the take. George would just quietly tell the assistant director to put her more to the side and do another take."[43]

Shelley Winters was

Top and bottom: Taking a nap in Berlin during the filming of ***The Big Lift,*** 1949.

Top: Publicity shot from *A Place in the Sun* with Elizabeth Taylor and Shelley Winters, 1949. *Bottom:* With Shelley Winters in another publicity shot from the same film.

personally cast by George Stevens, who had been convinced by her talent and determination since her screen test, where she showed up dressed in old clothes and without make-up. "It was a pleasure to work with Monty, I had the sensation that I knew him well already," she would later say. For his part, Monty was dissatisfied with his costar, thinking of her as "downbeat, blubbery, irritating."[44] The script required a scene in which the characters swim in the cold waters of the lake, and Monty and Elizabeth Taylor were meant to have worn bathing suits. But Monty had never before shown his body, and according to Ben Bagley, he was very self-conscious and ashamed of his skinny legs and virtually non-existent behind, which he often padded.[45] Because Monty refused to undress, Stevens changed the scene by just having Taylor in her swimsuit, while Monty was lying down, fully clothed on the bank of the river observing her swimming.

The relationship between Monty and Elizabeth was platonic, yet intimate. She was the first to foresee the greatness of his acting:

> I remember thinking, here I am working with Montgomery Clift, a genu-ine stage actor. Naturally I didn't know what Method meant, but it sounded serious. So I thought, I'm going to be serious too, by God! He had a coach and I did not understand that because I had never ever had acting lessons, much less a coach.... Monty was the most emotional actor I ever worked with and it is contagious. When he would start to shake, I would start to shake. Monty and Richard (Burton) give to the degree that it is almost a physical thing, like an umbilical cord, an electricity that goes back and forth.[46]

From Monty, Elizabeth learned the importance of introspection: the value of joining intuition and spontaneity with an interior quiet so that whatever there was of her character in herself could be called to the surface

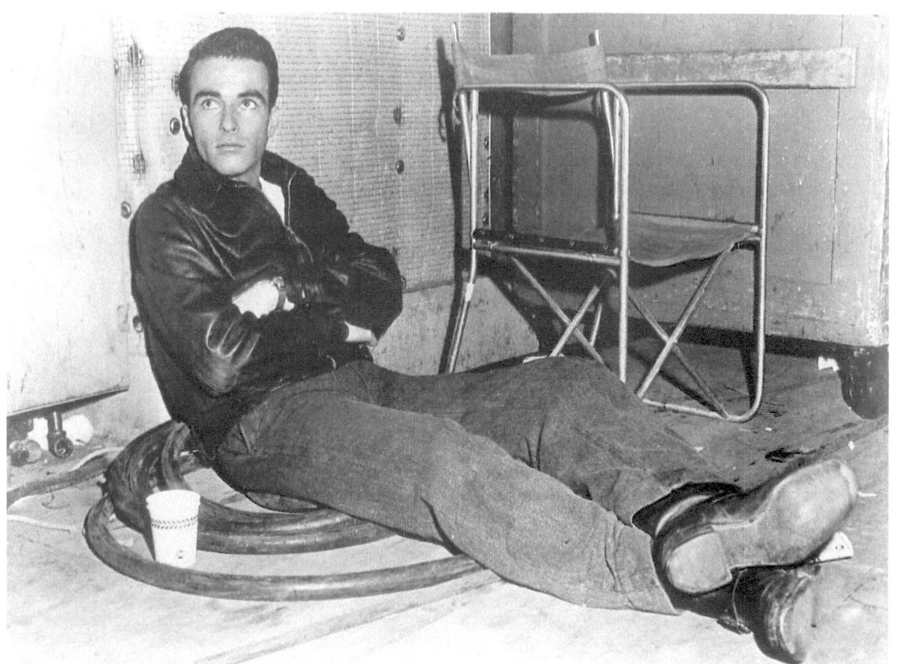

On the set of *A Place in the Sun*, 1949.

immediately by concentrating.[47] "In *A Place in the Sun* it was the first time I considered acting before it was only an extension of myself.... The hardest scene was when I had to say good-bye to Monty and to keep from crying.... Monty was one of the most important people in my life, he was my closest friend until he died. We really loved each other in the purest, in the most complete sense of the word."[48]

Top: Monty and Elizabeth Taylor in another publicity shot for *A Place in the Sun,* 1949. *Bottom:* The two in a scene from the same film.

A lot has been said and rumored about the nature of the relationship between Elizabeth and Monty. Apparently, it was never sexually consummated, although Elizabeth often upset Monty by teasing him about the way in which he made love. He often would tell her that he was too old for her, even as a friend (he was twelve years her senior). Other times he would act the part of the passionate male, making her believe he could fall in love with her. The next day, though, he would show up on the set with some young boy whom he had obviously picked up the night before.

Riding horses on location with Elizabeth Taylor on the set of *A Place in the Sun,* 1949.

"I knew he was gay, probably even more than he did," Taylor said. "And I helped him with it. Which is extraordinary because I was only about sixteen, and I really didn't know anything about it. I turned seventeen during the filming of the movie. I really didn't know then what being a homosexual was. But I just knew … well, I don't know how I knew…."[49]

It was this great sense of mutual understanding and maturity that bonded Elizabeth and Monty together in a lifetime friendship.

Stevens took advantage of their intimacy and shot one of the most extraordinary love scenes, among them a memorable close-up in which Elizabeth maternally whispers to him, "Tell mama … tell mama all." "I wanted to get the feeling of them both being totally lost in each other," recalled the director.[50]

Paramount knew that it was the right time to make the "love story" public. Using a clever publicity stunt, they announced a future wedding between Montgomery Clift and Elizabeth Taylor. Monty was very upset by the news and blamed Hollywood columnist Hedda Hopper for spreading

A candid shot taken during his trip in Europe.

the false story, but the real culprits were George Stevens and Paramount. For her part, Elizabeth did not care too much, she was going out with Nicky Hilton, the 23-year-old son of international hotelier Conrad Hilton. Soon after she would marry him, despite Monty's dislike for him and his belief that he was a womanizer and a ruthless gambler.

After four months of shooting, Monty was so exhausted that he not only turned down Stevens' next film, *Shane,* but also a Broadway production of *Hamlet* starring Katharine Hepburn as Gertrude. First he went to visit Libby Holman at Treetop for a couple of days, and then he left with Mira for Acapulco, to relax away all the tension and stress that had accumulated from work. "It is OVER. At last I can afford to collapse. Oy — I never thought this day would come,"[51] he wrote in a letter to Brooks.

His inactivity lasted longer than he expected. He went more than two years without making a movie, something that would have been impossible if he had been under a contract with any studio.

During the time off, Monty returned to the idea of writing the script for *You Touched Me!* with Kevin McCarthy. The two friends left together for a long trip to Europe. In Paris they went to a concert at the Étoile of the French singer Yves Montand, and they went to see legendary Arletty in Jean Cocteau's production of *A Streetcar Named Desire.* Monty also met with Thornton Williams and spent an entire day with him talking about literature. The playwright advised him to read *Diary of a Thief* by Jean Genet, whose work he appreciated a lot.

But in Europe, it was Italy that again impressed Monty the most. "What I like about Italy is [that it has] the most places there [that] are timeless. The people, many of them poor as they are, have a graceful, mellow zest for living. They are more proud of tradition and antiquity than they are of ambition and their modern postwar buildings."[52]

In Milan, Monty met Italian filmmaker Vittorio De Sica, who was shooting *Miracle in Milan.* Monty was a big fan of all of De Sica's work, especially *Shoeshine* and *The Bicycle Thieves,* which surprised the Italian director. They had lunch together in a little tavern where De Sica told him of his passion for gambling, and about how much he would have liked to make a movie based on a story about one of those old, rich, lonely ladies, who spend all night gambling in the casinos. "Gamblers feel their fortunes, their destinies are told in money," De Sica told him. They promised to keep in touch with one other, and would make a movie together a couple of years later.[53]

In Rome, Monty and the McCarthys stayed at the Hotel Savoia in Via Ludovisi, where they met Tennessee Williams, who introduced them to the aristocrat movie director Luchino Visconti. In Visconti's villa, Monty and the McCarthys were impressed by his beautiful antique pieces and by the lushness of the garden. During dinner they met Visconti's young assistant, Franco Zeffirelli, who was one of Monty's admirers. As he later stated in his autobiography, Zeffirelli tried to model himself after Monty and would imitate him in front of the mirror for hours.[54] The three friends were also invited to Visconti's costume ball, in which Roman nobility and high society members participated. Zeffirelli painted a beard on Monty's face and gave him a turban so that he would look like a fakir.

After their sojourn in Rome, they reached Naples, where they stayed at the Hotel Excelsior in a room with a spectacular view overlooking the bay and the Vesuvius. From there, they took short excursions to the islands of Capri and Ischia and to Paestum, an old Greek colony south of Naples. Monty wanted to see everything from landscape to arts. Last stop on the way back was Florence, where Kevin took some photographs of him hanging from the balcony of the hotel pretending to jump into the Arno River. From Dante's city, Monty mailed many postcards to Elizabeth Taylor, answering each of the daily letters she had written to him.

The only negative aspect of the long vacation was Monty's addiction to pills of all types and colors. When Augusta McCarthy asked him what they were for, he replied that they helped him to feel better and provided no further explanation.

Coming back to New York on the *Queen Elizabeth*, Kevin again took a photograph of Monty in another dangerous prank: during a wind storm, he pretended to walk home on the waters of the Atlantic, with just one hand on the railing of the liner, keeping him from an icy death.

Back home, things between Monty and Kevin did not go very well, especially regarding the writing of the screenplay *You Touched Me!* Monty was always unhappy with it, continuously changing the dialogue and believing that every line seemed wrong. The effects of his heavy drinking and use of pills were the cause of this.

"The result was terrible," remembers Donald Windham, who co-wrote the original play with Tennessee Williams. "The script was full of vulgar lines and the story was boring and dull."[55]

When Monty sent it to different producers, the answers he received back were not at all promising: 20th Century–Fox thought it was slow, United Artists found it tasteless and Columbia Pictures called it boring and repetitive.[56]

F O U R

Star

"His hazel eyes were so beautiful that when
he laughed, I just felt I'd moved a mountain."
— *Franklin Macfie*

Monty felt very discouraged and decided to spend that summer in Cape Cod, where he rented the house of Kevin's sister, writer Mary McCarthy. He turned the house into a pigsty because he would do everything on the floor: eat, drink, smoke and take pills with some friends in an atmosphere of total decadence.

One night when he was quite drunk, he started to scream out rambling sentences to his boyfriend "Rick" while in the presence of the guy's brother, thus revealing their secret relationship. The two brothers dragged him down to the ocean and gave him a good dunking just to shut him up.[1]

All of his close friends started to worry about him, and they advised him to see Dr. Ruth Fox, a psychiatrist who specialized in the treatment of alcoholics. After only a few months of group therapy, Monty decided to quit. One night, though, he collapsed blind drunk and Dr. Fox admitted him into Columbia-Presbyterian Hospital. The doctor was convinced that Monty's emotional problems were too complicated and deep for her to handle and decided to refer him, instead, to her colleague Dr. William Silverberg. Unfortunately, her choice ended up not being very fortunate for Monty's health.

Silverberg was fifty-three years old, married with children and gay. His teacher was Franz Alexander who had been Freud's pupil. It was Silverberg's idea that the key to perfect mental health was in what he called

69

Publicity shot, on the set of *I Confess*, 1952.

"effective aggression," a method of freely responding to one's own impulses and desires without the analysis of childhood-based problems. According to Silverberg, alcoholism and drug addiction were mere symptoms of a radical frustration in the patient's existence. In the beginning, the almost daily sessions within the beautiful, Central Park West office seemed to have some results, but the long-term effects were completely negative.

Over the course of 14 years of therapy (which Sunny Clift called a "total waste of money"), Monty became completely dependent upon the questionable theories of his psychiatrist. Billy LeMassena remembers: "I think we were all shocked at the speed with which Monty's addictions had caught hold. But this man Silverberg was no good influence at all; as it developed, it was clear to everyone that he was actually encouraging Monty into excesses, rather than preventing them."[2]

Monty also continued to behave in a strange manner sexually. He was going out with an Italian guy, a former pilot for a major airline, whom he met in a restaurant while the man was waiting tables. None of Monty's close friends liked this new boyfriend, who had an American wife and who was culturally inferior to him. But Monty was completely disinterested in those details. Besides, he often went to a notorious gay bar on East 51st Street, where he was picking up all kinds of men whom he would regularly bring home.

His casual sexual liaisons became such a frequent habit that he had to change his telephone number several times in order to avoid annoying calls that he received at every hour of the day and the night. Some of these calls contained threats of blackmail. It was a difficult time for Monty, who was jobless for over a year and who was collecting unemployment, despite the fact that he did not actually need it. But as his friend Donald Windham remembers, he was never ashamed of this because he thought it was a government's duty to help unemployed, professional actors.[3]

Meantime, Monty moved into a duplex apartment at 209 East 61st Street, not too far from Libby Holman's residence.

In August 1950, he traveled back to London for the British gala premiere of *The Heiress*. Hundreds of fans besieged the Connaught Hotel, where he was staying. Monty had dinner with Laurence Olivier and was formally introduced to Queen Elizabeth, along with actors Tyrone Power and James Stewart.

Then he went to Rome, where during a press-conference he met 25-year-old Italian columnist Giovanni

Publicity shot, on the set of *I Confess,* 1952.

Perrone, who wrote the gossip column "Roman Holiday" in a newspaper called *Il Progresso*. One day Perrone was witness to a strange episode that happened in the actor's hotel suite.

While the journalist was having a drink with Monty, a beautiful blonde delivering a bouquet of roses knocked at the door. As soon as Monty opened it, she removed her fur coat, and stood there naked, offering herself to him. Monty was puzzled, then quickly remembering who was paying for the hotel room, he realized that she was a "present" from Paramount, which was attempting to bolster his dubious heterosexuality. Monty called the people from the production. Protesting angrily, he complained that his sexual life was nobody's business but his.[4]

The production tour for *The Heiress* was supposed to continue on to Milan and Paris, but it was abruptly interrupted by Monty. He returned home, without giving Paramount any notice, when he heard the news that Topper Holman, Libby's son, had died while he was climbing Mount Whitney in California.

This tragedy enormously shocked Monty. Libby was still one of his

A beautiful portrait of Monty, early 1950s.

most intimate friends and a neighbor and a great host for several weekends at Treetops, even though many friends thought that this relationship was not especially healthy for him. According to writer Paul Bowles, author of *The Sheltering Sky,* "Monty was one of the least happy people he had ever known and it made him uncomfortable to be in his company ... especially when he was with Libby. There was too much drinking, too much self doubt, too much introspection and it was bad for both of them."[5] Jack Larson, who had achieved fame by portraying Jimmy Olsen, the cub photographer for the *Daily Planet* in the television series of Superman, was a close friend of Monty's and believed that Libby's romantic obsession with him was purely masochistic. She was always choosing men to dominate, and at the same time she identified with their agony.[6]

Monty turned down all the scripts that he read during this time, with the exception of *From Here to Eternity*. He was very excited about the possibility of being part of such a production. *From Here to Eternity* was based on the best-selling novel by James Jones. Monty met the author at a party, attended by many intellectuals, given by literary critic Vance Bourjaily in his Greenwich Village apartment. Jones told Monty that he would have been perfect for the role of Prewitt, even though Columbia Pictures' head Harry Cohn, who held the film rights, wanted the part for John Derek. Monty was not sure that he would be able to act the part of an ex-boxer, but Jones' enthusiasm swept him away. The project, though, took a long time before coming to life, and the movie went into production one year later.

In August 1951 *A Place in the Sun* opened in the American theaters. It grossed over $3 million at the box office, reaching the 8th position in the annual chart. The *New York Times* wrote that the film was "a work of beauty, tenderness, power and insight" and "Montgomery Clift's portrayal,

Monty with Nancy Balaban (Paramount Pictures President Barney Balaban's daughter) and an unidentified interviewer, at the premiere of *A Place in the Sun* at the Capitol Theatre in New York, 1951.

often terse and hesitating, is full, rich, restrained and above all, generally credible and poignant."[7] For one of the screenings of the movie, Monty flew to Dallas where he met with his sister and old friend, Lehman Engel, who was the musical conductor of the State Fair Musicals.[8]

The night of the New York premiere at the Capitol theater, Monty arrived accompanied by 18-year-old Judy Balaban, the daughter of the president of Paramount Pictures, Barney Balaban. "He was very much like an older brother in many ways ... I was certainly in love with him and he with me," Judy remembered. "We spent almost a year together.... We did speak of getting married but we spoke about it more in a sense of playfulness."[9]

However, Judy soon realized that Monty had an energy that was moving him toward a different kind of life, something of which she could never be a part. Because of the little interest Monty showed in committing to a serious relationship with her and because of the strong opposition that came from her father against a union with a non–Jewish actor, the platonic romance eventually transformed into a nice friendship.

She introduced Monty to Merv Griffin (at the time just Balaban's friend, but someone who would later become her boyfriend) during a dinner in New York. Merv ordered a lemon meringue pie and Monty stuck his finger into it to taste it. Playing to the staring crowd, he began to lick the meringue off the pie. Griffin did not find this amusing, so with both hands he shoved Monty's face flush into the pie. "He looked up, the face that thrilled America on the screen a gooey mess of meringue and lemon filling," Griffin later wrote. "Slowly he wiped the pie off his face. He said quietly, 'Yeah that's good pie, Merv. You're right, it's really good pie.' From that moment on we were friends."[10]

Judy Balaban was not the only one who became a victim of his charm. Tons of teenagers crowded movie theaters to watch Elizabeth Taylor and Montgomery Clift in *A Place in the Sun,* the most beautiful couple in cinema history, as reported by all American magazines. A fan club started in his honor, and he was constantly besieged by hordes of hysterical teenagers. Among these was Franklin Macfie, an 18-year-old boy, who after watching the movie started to stalk Monty. He found out where the actor lived and followed him for several years.[11] "It was not difficult to spot him," Macfie said; "he was often drinking in a bar at the corner of 51st Street and Lexington Avenue.[12]

One day Macfie approached his idol telling him, "This is who I am and you are going to see this face a lot. Get used to seeing this face following you."[13] Monty did not pay too much attention to the crazy fan until the day Macfie showed up at this house, pretending to deliver a package. "The maid let me in, and he was up on the third floor in the bedroom, and in the living room the television was on. He was a big baseball fan, strangely enough…. And he came downstairs. I was adjusting the television set; which was flickering, and he was wearing gray khaki pants and a white T-shirt. He looked quizzically at me and he said, 'What are you doing here?' And I said, 'Oh I'm fixing the television, as you can see.' And he smiled and we started talking. Nothing happened at the time."

A couple of months later they had sex together. "I think three times. Once on the staircase…. He was the most beautiful creature I ever saw in my life. Monty was for the eyes. It was the eyes and to get a laugh. He was one of those people that if you could get him in to laugh, to really actually laugh at something, you felt you had achieved some great catharsis for him. I just felt I'd moved a mountain."[14]

In that year Monty broadcast two radio programs: a short drama entitled *The Metal of the Moon,* which was part of a serial called *The Cavalcade*

Monty "cruising" in a gay bar in the Upper East Side in New York, in a photograph taken by a paparazzo for a tabloid in the mid–1950s.

of America, and an adaptation of Tennessee Williams' 1945 play *The Glass Menagerie* with legendary co-star Helen Hayes. Monty took several weeks off just to analyze the script, memorize it and pick it apart. When the time came to broadcast, he could relate to every other actor in the program and he was able to perform without looking at the script.[15]

Monty received an unexpected visit from Elizabeth Taylor, who was looking for some comfort from her friend because she was on the verge of breaking up with Nicky Hilton. They spent many hours together, having dinner at Camillo's, their favorite Italian restaurant, where they often chatted past closing time, or went to clubs, often in company of a new friend, young actor Roddy McDowall, who would become one of Monty's close friends.

Elizabeth was staying at the Plaza Hotel, which belonged to the chain of hotels owned by the husband she was divorcing. The management of the hotel sent a $3000 bill to her, stating that they never received any different instruction of payment. Elizabeth was furious, and with the help of Monty and Roddy, she messed up the suite and secretly left the hotel without paying the bill. They unscrewed each of the door and window handles, and they knocked the vases over onto the tapestry, ruining the floor and carpet. They also took all the towels from the bathroom. The day after this, the incident was reported in some newspapers. Before going back to Los Angeles, Elizabeth stayed with Monty for a couple of extra days.

The following summer Monty went back to work and acted in *I Confess,* a film directed by Alfred Hitchcock. He was very excited about the idea of portraying a priest, because the subject of holiness and martyrdom had always fascinated him a great deal. A couple of years prior to this he had met Brother Thomas, a young priest with whom he stayed in touch by trading lively correspondence. Before reaching the set, Monty asked him if he could visit as a guest in his monastery. For five days he acquainted himself with the religious life, learning the Latin Mass and the Via Crucis stations. He observed: "Monks' passion for saints is like ours for movie stars."

The filming for *I Confess* started first in Hollywood, where Monty stayed at the Greens. In those days he was almost arrested for driving in a drunken state, but thanks to his charm and fame, he merely got a ticket. Shooting proceeded on schedule without major incidents, except for the defection of screenwriter Paul Tabori, who walked out after an argument with Hitchcock about the end of the film. Tabori's intention was to write a suspenseful drama in which a young priest, Father Logan, is wrongly accused of a murder. He can only free himself by violating the sanctity of the confessional. The priest is blackmailed by the real murderer, who threatens to reveal a relationship he had with a married woman before joining the religious order. The original ending of the script had the priest sentenced to the death penalty, but Hitchcock chose a happy ending, instead, perhaps worried about the refusal of the Roman Catholic Church to cooperate with the filming if the priest was to be executed.

Swedish actress Anita Björk was first cast as the leading female role, but she arrived in Hollywood with a live-in lover and an illegitimate child. Remembering the recent scandal caused by Ingrid Bergman, who left her husband to have a child with Italian director Roberto Rossellini, Warner Bros. decided to offer the part to Olivia de Havilland, who turned it down. So, they signed on Anne Baxter. The actress had just achieved fame with her great performance in *All About Eve.* She had been supposed to co-star with Monty in *The Adventures of Tom Saywer,* but he had been forced to refuse due to a bad case of acne.

Even though Karl Malden was not under contract with Warner Bros., Monty helped him get the part of Inspector Larrue. The actor remembers in his autobiography: "Monty was perfect for the priest; he had the face of a saint but when you looked into his eyes you saw a tortured soul, trying to make its way out of utter bewilderment."[16] Malden was the only actor in the cast who Monty would see off the set, but he would often get upset with him because Malden did not act the same way that he did when they rehearsed together just the night before.

Filming resumed in Quebec City, a location chosen not only for its beautiful setting but also because it was the only place in North America where priests had always worn the frock, a key element in identifying the suspect in the plot of the movie. The cast and the crew were accommodated at the Hotel Château Elysée, while Hitchcock resided at the luxurious Château Frontenac.

Mira Rostova's presence was a great cause of tension. Karl Malden said, "Monty depended on her, kept a distance from Hitchcock and from the rest of

Monty wearing the frock as Father Logan in *I Confess,* 1952.

us to go over his lines with her, insisted on her approval before a scene could be shot. Naturally this created a deep division and tension."[17] During the filming of the scene where Father Logan refuses to reveal the murderer's identity to the inspector, Monty and Malden interacted very intensely. Hitchcock, characteristically impassive, was visibly moved and jumped up from his chair proclaiming, "Brilliant! Print it." Merv Griffin said, "Clift looked at Mira who made a signal by putting a hand on her left ear. When the applause died down, Monty asked to do the scene over. Hitchcock whirled, trembling with rage and glared at Mira. But the scene was shot again. And somehow improved."[18]

Anne Baxter recalls: "Poor Monty was drinking so heavily, virtually all the time"[19] and Hitchcock quickly noticed the difficulty of dealing with such a complex personality and with an actor too obscure in his methods.[20] The director was annoyed with Monty's introspective approach to the role and with his refusal to collaborate with the rest of the cast. At the same time, however, he was fascinated with his private life, his sexual ambiguity and his tormented psychology.[21]

Upon the completion of *I Confess,* Hitchcock wanted to finish off the already drunk Monty, and dared him to drink a full beaker of brandy. Anne

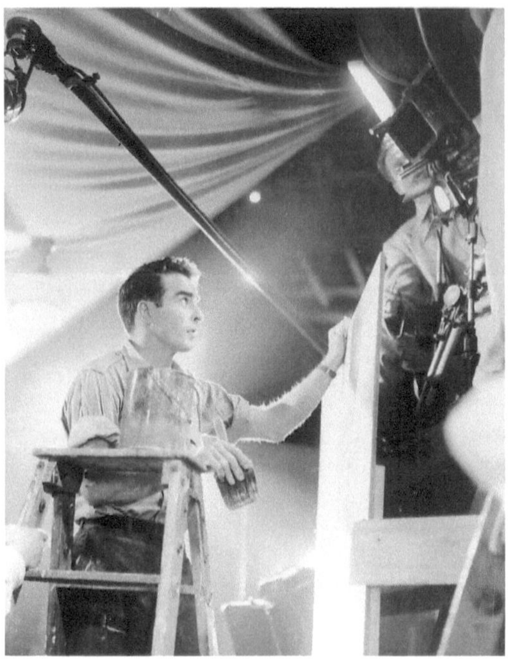

On the set of Hitchcock's *I Confess,* 1952 (Ken Galente Collection).

Baxter and Karl Malden watched motionless and horrified. Monty drank, and a moment later fell to the floor, face down in a dangerous alcoholic stupor, while Hitchcock observed with sadistic pleasure. Upon meeting the director again 20 years later, Malden asked him to explain exactly what had happened that night. As Hitchcock recounted a disgusting scene in which Monty had used the backseat of his rented car as a bathroom in every possible way, the actor noticed the same pleasure in the director's eyes that he had seen that night years before. "It was a pathetic sight. This great talent who could have been our country's Gielgud, who should have played Romeo, Hamlet and all those parts that require the class he had naturally. Instead slowly so slowly he simply lost control…. But when we were working together you could already sense that his life was an accident waiting to happen."[22]

While in Quebec, Monty was visited by Vittorio De Sica, who wanted him to star in *Stazione Termini,* whose filming was scheduled to start the following December in Rome. The two friends chatted in French for a long time, and Monty disagreed with De Sica's idea to have an Italian actor who spoke English on the set to serve as an intermediary between the two of them, since De Sica did not speak English and Monty did not speak Italian. At the end, Monty accepted although he was not completely convinced.

That summer Monty asked Fred Green to redesign his brownstone on 61st Street. The renovation work lasted over four months and Monty specifically requested a custom-made, four by ten foot long mirrored medicine cabinet. Its contents would become almost legendary due to the various types of medication and countless bottles of pills which he kept in it.

While the construction work was in progress, Monty was a guest in Libby Holman's apartment, only one block away. Each day Jeanne Green would go furniture shopping for him and on more than one occasion, she was astounded by Monty's bizarre behavior. Once, Monty urinated in the elevator of Hammacher's department store, justifying his behavior by saying that he did not know where the men's room was. Other times he would ask her to leave him alone because he had to meet with the "Gangster," a nickname for a Bronx drug dealer, who was providing him with all of the pills he needed.

Suddenly, Monty was becoming bossy with his friends. One night he bought some tickets for a show for all his friends except Fred Green, because he wanted him to keep working on the renovation of his apartment. Green felt like he was being exploited, and did not recognize Monty as the usual generous friend he used to know. Upon the completion of the work, Monty again offended the couple by giving his friend an ugly watch engraved with the dedication "To a timeless friend" as a compensation for his work. It was an old Christmas present he had received from a film agent.

In October 1952 Monty made the first and only political speech of his career. It was on the eve of the presidential election and he decided to support the Democratic candidate, Adlai Stevenson, at a rally held at Madison Square Garden. Humphrey Bogart, Lauren Bacall, Robert Ryan and Tallulah Bankhead also joined him. Brooks accompanied his brother, while their father, a fervent Republican, was outraged at the idea of his son endorsing the Democratic candidate. A furious argument ensued between father and son, one which resumed after years of a lack of mutual understanding. Bill told Monty not to speak to him again and not to be at his funeral, resulting in a hard and very painful separation.

One month later, Monty arrived in Rome to start *Stazione Termini*. One of his first Italian social events was to receive the Nastro d'Argento award (Silver Ribbon) as best foreign actor for *A Place in the Sun*. He was traveling with his lover "Dino," who had substituted omnipresent Mira Rostova. Monty felt this time that he was not in need of a coach, completely trusting in De Sica's direction.

The producer of *Stazione Termini* was the legendary and bossy David Selznick, whose fame was connected to *Gone with the Wind*. He believed that Italian Neorealism was an important phenomenon related to the entire worldwide film industry. In the past, he had tried to convince director Roberto Rossellini to participate in a joint project, and then he bought the story for the movie from Italian writer Cesare Zavattini.

Originally, French director Autant-Lara was chosen to make the movie, but when he visited the railroad station in Rome, he was frightened by the dimension and requested that it be rebuilt on a set in Cinecittà. Selznick categorically refused. Meantime, a long series of famous writers started to work on the original story, attempting to adapt it into a screen-play: From Zavattini, the original writer, to Paul Gallico, to Alberto Moravia to Carson McCullers, to Truman Capote. Capote arrived in Rome the same day as Monty, and he claimed to have written only two scenes in the final film version.

Stazione Termini tells of the last hours of a passionate love story inside a Roman train station between the lovers Giovanni Doria, a young Italian professor (played by Monty) and Mary Forbes, an elegant, American housewife (played by Jennifer Jones, Selznick's wife). The movie ran many little subplots, vignettes about other travelers in the station, all portrayed by popular Italian actors.

"The railroad station was available for filming only at night," recalled De Sica in an interview. "The normal daily schedule would finish around half past midnight. Only then could we film and start everything again: trains, travelers, shops, porters, workers, etc. We spent 75 consecutive nights without sleeping and barely eating."[23]

Great chemistry was established between Jennifer Jones and Monty, because he was very similar to Robert Walker, Jones' first husband who had recently died. He was sensitive, moody and emotional but at the same time capable of manipulating people with great ability. The actress fell in love with him and gave him an expensive Gucci briefcase as a present. Jones was taken by total surprise when she heard her co-star was gay. Monty used to joke with his friends about Jennifer's gift because one of the clasps turned out to be broken, saying, "It is beautiful but it doesn't work — how like Jennifer!"[24]

The truth was that Jones was going through a bad time with her husband, quarrelling throughout the production. Once she was so upset with him that she threw into the toilet a mink hat which she was supposed to wear in the movie. The hat was part of her wardrobe, exclusively designed by Christian Dior. Another time she ran back to the hotel barefooted, followed by her husband's limo, leaving De Sica and the set in a situation in which it was impossible to film. On another occasion she lost her temper with Selznick while she was shooting a love scene with Monty. The producer was constantly interrupting to make personal changes to the take. Outraged, Jennifer violently slapped her husband, breaking his glasses; Selznick was practically blind without them.

More problems on the set were simply related to miscommunication. De Sica spoke Italian and French, Monty spoke English and French, Jennifer Jones and David Selznick just spoke English. The constant presence of translators did not ease the situation at all. Monty always had little notes in his pockets with his Italian lines often misspelled.

A scene from Vittorio De Sica's *Indiscretion of an American Wife* with Jennifer Jones, 1953.

Truman Capote remembers:

> Monty was really gifted. He was serious about only one thing, and that thing was acting. He was an exception to my theory that a movie star has to be ignorant to be good. You have to be smart to be on the stage, but a film actor is just a conduit for the writer, the director and everybody else who puts something into the picture. He has to react to what they do.... Monty was smart and good, but that was because he was also very shrewd: he knew just what he was doing. I once asked him why he wanted to act in movies, why he didn't do something more interesting. He looked at me and said, "You don't understand. It's my life. This is what I know to do." He was an artist, with all of an artist's sensibilities and flaws.[25]

Soon Monty started to become stressed by the uncomfortable atmosphere on the set. He wrote a little note in broken Italian, found inside his personal copy of the script where he says: "Io arriva Italia, io una settimana strapazzato. Io due settimane pazzo (I arrive Italy. I one week very tired. I two weeks crazy)."[26]

In a letter to his brother Brooks he described the fatigue of filming

Strolling in Rome on the Spanish Steps, 1953.

by night. "It's hell over here. We shoot out of doors in the station from 10:30 to 7 am. By one o'clock everybody is numb from cold and by three the hacking and coughing and spitting and general wheezing is so all-pervasive that it is almost impossible to shoot a scene with sound. I won't get a day off until Xmas, so I have no time to recover. I'm not praying to be healthy but only to live until 1953 — Please God."[27]

Off the set Monty was still drinking, probably because he was having problems with his lover, who was cheating on him while he was filming. Truman Capote did not understand why Monty was involved with "such an asshole." Shortly afterward, Monty finally broke up with his "pilot." Although Monty was never fond of effeminate men, his friendship with Capote was an exception; in fact, he was an admirer of his writing style. In a long interview with De Sica, writer Charles Thomas Samuels observed that among all the problems that the film had, there was also the fact that Monty did not seem masculine enough and that some of the dialogue written by Capote did not give the right impression, either. De Sica agrees with the interviewer saying, "Yes they were both pederasts."[28]

Problems resumed after the completion of the film, which lasted a total of just over two months. The censorship committee was made up of Italians and Americans. As De Sica recalls, "What was working and fine for the Italians was not good for Americans and vice versa. It was a real mess."[29] Therefore, Selznick changed the title for the American market, releasing the film as *Indiscretion of an American Wife*. He made over an hour of cuts and accompanied the movie with a short film featuring singer

Patti Page. During the editing of the film, the producer also added many close-ups of his wife, further altering the original film.

De Sica's picture was presented at the 1953 Cannes Film Festival, but it was not a success. It was not a success at the box office either, in any country. It earned less than $1 million in North America.

Perturbed Spirit

"Monty led many lives, we were only part of one of them."
— *Jeanne Green*

While in Rome, Monty confirmed with writer James Jones that he had been cast as Private Prewitt in *From Here to Eternity*.

Dear Jones —

I guess you know I'm going to play your boy Prewitt. I never believed it would happen when I met you. I'd like to know where the Hell I could reach you when I get back to the States — which will be early in January. I don't care where you are — I'd like to talk to you. Will you write me either here or at home: 149 East 61st — NYC?

I'd like to impose on you to the extent of plaguing you with questions for a day.

Please write.

Monty Clift[1]

Fred Zinnemann was chosen to direct the film by Columbia's bossy president Harry Cohn. The director wanted Monty as Prewitt (preferring him to John Derek and Aldo Ray, Cohn's first choices). "I wanted Clift because this story was not about a fellow who didn't want to box: it was about a man who resists all sorts of pressure from an institution he loves, who becomes an outsider and eventually dies for it. It was clear to me, if difficult to explain, what Clift would make of that character."[2]

Monty had to shave his hirsute chest for his role of Private Prewitt in *From Here to Eternity,* 1953.

Monty was ecstatic. He went to visit James Jones in Tucson, Arizona, to talk about how he should prepare himself for this role. During those four days, Jones noticed that Monty was carefully observing him, paying particular attention to his gestures, his movements and his nervous tics, which were the result of a long training period spent in the Army that built his character. Monty was awed by Jones the writer, as well as Jones the military man.[3]

While in Los Angeles, Monty went to the gym every day to keep fit and to make his body more muscular. He also shaved his hairy chest, which for the first time would be shown bare on the screen. He jogged and studied boxing with former junior welterweight champion Mushy Calahan, who had coached Kirk Douglas for *Champion* and Burt Lancaster for *Jim Thorpe — All American.*

Monty learned to play the bugle from well-known musician Manny Klein, even though he knew that all the bugling on the soundtrack would be dubbed by a professional musician. Nevertheless, he wanted his mouth and throat movements to look as natural as possible. For weeks he looked in every Los Angeles music store trying to find the same type of crystal mouthpiece described in the book, but it was no longer made so he had to be pleased with one that was similar. While in Hollywood, he preferred to stay in the low budget Roosevelt Hotel far from Beverly Hills. He would practice playing the bugle daily, often provoking many complaints by other hotel guests. Today a legend circulates that room 928, used by Monty during the filming, is haunted, and it is said that hotel guests can hear his voice pronouncing his lines.[4]

Monty was accompanied by Mira Rostova, even though Dr. Silverberg had told him to slowly distance himself from her. One day they had a heated argument regarding the psychiatrist, and Monty was very upset and drank heavily. He decided not to deal with her ever again. Mira was extremely preoccupied by Monty's furious, overreaction. In a panic, she called Dr. Silverberg, but the specialist told her not to interfere because the situation was under control. At that moment, Mira got an unpleasant sense of foreboding that something terrible would happen but she still decided to return to New York.

Burt Lancaster, who was in the movie recalled:

> I remember so well the first scene I did with Montgomery Clift. It was the first time — the only time this ever happened to me in my entire experience — that I could not stop my knees from shaking.
>
> He had so much power, so much concentration. Thank God the camera was only shooting above my waist. But after that it was fine and we became very good friends. Clift was a complicated man, there's no question about that. He and Frank Sinatra would get roaring drunk every night after filming. I spent so much time carrying them into bed night after night.[5]

But Monty's feelings for Lancaster were completely different. He thought he was a "terrible actor" and a "big bag of wind," perhaps because Lancaster got a higher salary than he did. With Zinnemann the situation was different. The relationship was based on mutual collaboration and affection perhaps because they had previously worked together. Monty also had good feelings for his favorite idol, singer Frank Sinatra, whose bald attitude toward life he tremendously admired.

Shortly Sinatra became a fan of Monty's and followed all his advice on improving his acting. "With Montgomery I had to be patient because I knew that if I watched this guy, I'd learn something. We had a mutual admiration thing goin' there."[6] But during an interview on the *Hy Gardner Show* in the 1960's, Monty told the show's host that he never had to help Sinatra during *From Here to Eternity*, because he was a natural born actor. "I couldn't help him, but he

Monty practicing the bugle with well-known trumpeter Manny Klein, 1953.

helped me, with the trumpet business and marching properly. Sinatra can do anything."[7]

A rumor developed that Sinatra, whose acting career was stalling, used "influential friends" to obtain the role. Zinnemann never sustained the rumor and maintained that Sinatra got the part only because his screen test was good and he accepted a modest $8000 salary.

Monty, Sinatra and James Jones used to be inseparable and would go and have dinner in a little Italian

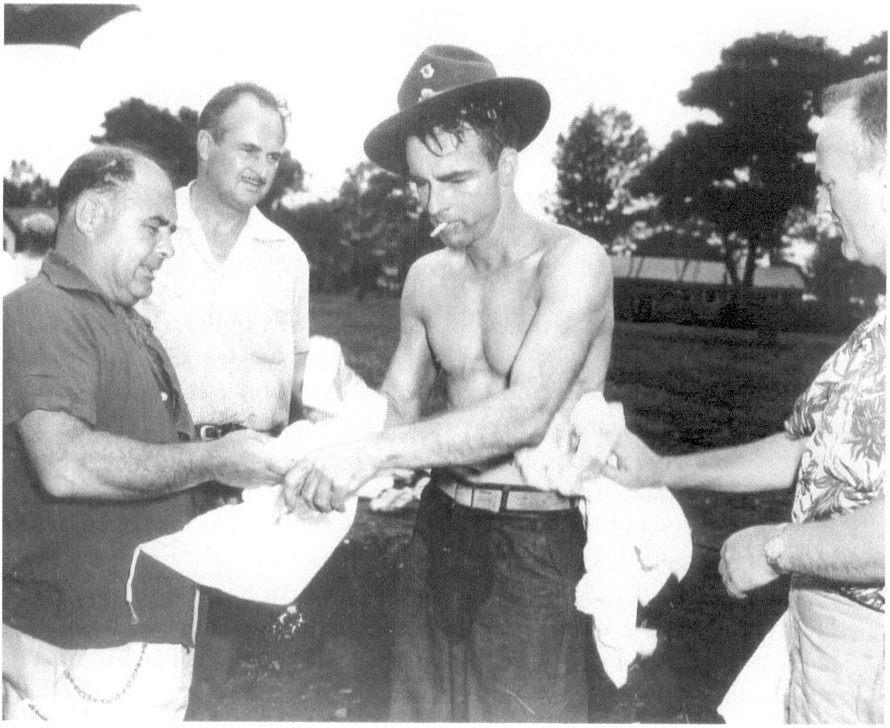

Top: Monty played the bugle for hours to perfect movements of his mouth and throat. *Bottom:* With the film's crew between takes of *From Here to Eternity,* 1953.

With Burt Lancaster in a scene from *From Here to Eternity*, 1953.

restaurant owned by the singer's friend in West Hollywood. Jones remembers those wild nights talking about the unfairness of life and about love, in addition to listening to the endless stories Sinatra would tell about Ava Gardner, who was his wife at the time and who was working in Africa, filming *Mogambo*. Monty and Jones would keep him company while he was trying to reach Gardner on the phone, and they would often cheer him up after the frequent quarrels he had with her.

The trio would often go back to the Roosevelt Hotel completely drunk and twice they would have been kicked out if Columbia had not intervened. Monty's friendship with Sinatra did not last long. One night after the completion of *From Here to Eternity*, at a party in Bel Air hosted by the singer, Monty made a pass at another guest and Sinatra ordered his bodyguards to throw him out of the house.[8] Nevertheless, the actor kept an inscribed photograph of the singer and a gold lighter that Sinatra had given him for Christmas which was engraved: "Merry, Merry, buddy boy, I'm with you all the way. Maggio." (Maggio was Sinatra's character name in *From Here to Eternity*.)

On the other hand, his friendship with Jones was substantially intellectual, although fake rumors circulated about Jones' homosexuality. When someone asked the writer to comment about these insinuations, he boldly answered: "I would have had an affair with him, but he never asked me."[9] They corresponded for a long time, always remaining good friends.

All of the exteriors were filmed at the exact locations described in the novel. Columbia submitted the script to the U.S. Army in order to obtain their collaboration, and they finally agreed to cooperate after some changes were made to the script, such as eliminating expressions that were too vulgar and explicit references to male and female prostitution. Some Army officers were chosen as technical advisors and the Schofield Barracks in Hawaii was made available for the shooting. Harry Cohn set a strict budget regarding money and time, deciding that the film would be shot in black and white in order to contain its cost.

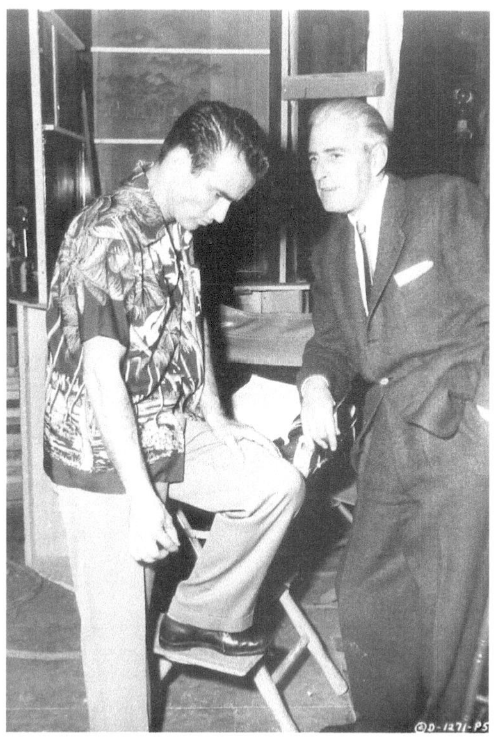

Talking through one of the scenes in *From Here to Eternity* with producer Buddy Adler, 1953.

Before leaving for Hawaii and upon completion of the filming at the studios in Hollywood, Monty went with the Greens for a long weekend to La Paz in Baja, California. Every night Monty would get roaring drunk by himself and would barely manage to find his way back to the hotel. The next day he would wake up with the shakes. (As one member of the cast put it, "When Monty drank, he seemed to lose his identity and almost melt before your eyes." During Angelo Maggio's death scene, Monty paradoxically "was too drunk even to play a drunk man."[10])

The chartered plane arrived at 5:00 a.m. on March 2, 1953; Frank and Monty were so drunk that Burt Lancaster and Deborah Kerr had to shake them to wake them up.[11] In Honolulu, the complete cast stayed at the

On the set of *From Here to Eternity* with Donna Reed and director Fred Zinnemann, 1953.

Alexander Young Hotel, and they often met in the evenings for dinner. When the conversation would drift away from the movie, Monty would change the subject back. Deborah Kerr was only in one scene with him, but she was visibly impressed by the fact that Monty rehearsed it for two entire days.

Donna Reed also remembers that she had never worked with an actor like him, who was so dedicated and charismatic and who had such a withering glance. At the same time he could shun other people's company.[12] Later Reed told her friend James Dean about the way Monty used to drive. "Everybody had to get out of Monty's way. He'd blow the horn — swerve this way and that, and he'd actually pull into the oncoming lane of traffic on a busy street to get around someone going too slow for Monty. And he passed cars on the right. What they call the 'suicide' side."[13]

From Here to Eternity premiered at New York's Capitol Theatre but with no more fanfare than a full page ad in the *New York Times*. But when the film opened everywhere at the end of the summer, it hit the box office and earned more than $12 million in the first few months of its release, while it cost only $2.5 million to make. Theaters had to be open all night to enable the huge crowd to watch it. The New York Critics Association awarded Zinnemann best director of the year, and he told the reporters at the ceremony, "I could not have gotten this without Monty."

From Here to Eternity obtained a record 13 Oscar nominations and won eight. Among them: Sinatra and Reed for best supporting actor and actress. Monty and Burt Lancaster lost the best actor to William Holden in *Stalag 17.* Monty was distraught that he did not win. He was sure that this was his chance after having lost twice before.

"What do I have to do to prove I can act?" he bitterly asked Howard Thompson of the *New York Times.* Perhaps, as Forster Hirsch wrote, Hollywood didn't want to feel his torment and alienation anymore. He would have to try to be "more of an actor" without being so real.[14] According to his agent Herman Citron, Monty was at the peak of his career: "He could have been the biggest movie star in the world. He was always considered before Brando, but he was

Top and bottom: At the pool table in *From Here to Eternity.*

Taking a pause with Deborah Kerr between takes of *From Here to Eternity*, 1953.

too choosy. We'd scream at each other over the phone. 'I will not do it, Herman,' he'd say. 'It's crap!' And I'd yell, 'Can't you lower your standards for once?'"[15]

In fact, Monty turned down scripts like *On the Waterfront, East of Eden, Desiree* that transformed other actors, like James Dean, into stars. Director Elia Kazan recalls that this new young actor, Dean, used to say that Montgomery Clift was his idol, his role model. Dennis Hopper added: "Jimmy used to call Monty Clift, when he was in New York and say: 'I'm a great actor, you are my idol, I need to see you because I need to communicate!' Monty was so annoyed that he changed his phone number."

A fact that greatly intrigued Monty was gossip about the screen test for *East of Eden* taken by Dean and Dick Davalos, who played the "good" brother, a part in which producers had originally cast Brando. The scene took place in Cal's (James Dean's) bedroom and it had so many explicit, homosexual overtones that it was cut from the final version. After Dean's premature death, Monty would watch each of this young actor's three films and get drunk and cry about the fact he had denied him the opportunity to see and talk to him.[16] Later, he discovered that Dean had also been a fan of Marlon Brando's and that he sometimes signed letters as "James (Brando Clift) Dean."

It seemed the right time for Monty to proceed with a long wished for collaboration project with Kevin McCarthy and Mira Rostova. The trio would work only for their personal pleasure. The play they chose was Chekhov's *The Sea Gull,* but they were not satisfied with any of the translations available, so they decided to do their own.

In Monty's apartment, Mira would translate the original Russian text word for word, while Monty and Kevin would adjust the words of the

A publicity shot with Donna Reed from *From Here to Eternity,* 1953.

literary translation into better and more incisive English. Mira maintained that she did most of the job with only Kevin's help because Monty was often away for a promotional tour for *From Here to Eternity.*

At the same time, director Norris Houghton and producer T. Edward Hambleton were setting up the off–Broadway Phoenix Theater based on the model of the Lyric in the London suburb of Hammersmith, a theater off the West End, where famous actors would play classic and other plays that were not too commercial. The old theater was situated in the East Village, and Houghton and Hambleton hoped that the Phoenix would one day have a repertory company like that of the Old Vic in London or the Abbey Theater in Ireland, a sort of unofficial American national theater.

When Houghton heard that Monty was setting up a new production of Chekhov's *The Sea Gull,* he called him right away. They had known each other since Monty had worked with him 16 years prior in *Dame Nature* when Houghton was a set designer. The director specified that the salary would not be high, but Monty accepted the offer, proposing Kevin and Mira for the parts of Trigorin and Nina, and himself as Treplieff, a playwright, who commits suicide after he has been turned down by the aspiring actress, Nina, who prefers the older and more cynical Trigorin to him.

The part of Madame Arkadina was the only one still uncast. Monty thought of his friend Marlene Dietrich, with whom he had always wanted to work. It seemed the perfect occasion because the running of the play would not last long, and afterwards she could go back to her film career. But Dietrich unexpectedly turned it down. Stella Adler was the second one to refuse the part, despite the fact that she seemed very interested. She had not played on stage for 10 years, which made her not feel confident enough to face such a demanding challenge. So, the part went to Judith Evelyn, who was a well-known name on Broadway after having acted with Vincent Price in *Angel Street*. Maureen Stapleton, an old friend of the trio, Sam Jaffe, George Voskovec, June Walker and Karl Light were cast in the play's secondary roles.

Just before the beginning of the rehearsals and during several meetings that he had with the cast to define details of the production, Houghton noticed how much Monty was drinking and how his concentration on work was often interrupted by the continuous calls from Elizabeth Taylor in California. "I was totally unfamiliar with symptoms of drug abuse … I attributed his high-strung state to increasing anxiety as we approached the rehearsals. After all, a lot was at stake for him: this was his first stage appearance since he had achieved Hollywood stardom. None of us could guess that it was to be his last."[17]

Maureen Stapleton remembers this subject. "I could not stand what was happening to that handsome man. He was getting worse. After a show one night, during a dinner party at Monty's, Monty was completely drunk and dropped to the ground. I started crying and told Roddy [McDowall]: 'We've got to do something. This can't go on; we've got to help him.' Roddy, one of the best people in the world, said very simply and sadly, 'The only thing we can do, Maureen, is hold his hand to the grave.'"[18]

What has been called the longest suicide in film history had just begun, and everybody realized this without understanding the reason why.

Monty wanted Arthur Miller to direct the play, but the playwright preferred to assume only the role of production advisor, contributing his personal opinions.

The Sea Gull was directed by Houghton with the promise that he would allow the actors to direct themselves freely as often as they liked. This freedom quickly became cause for argument, and Monty was so disappointed with Mira's acting that he was about to give up. She was probably a better teacher and coach than an actress. According to her, she made the mistake of agreeing to play a character too young for her age. In addition, the acoustics of the theater were not very good because the stage was too big for that kind of play.[19] Also, Karl Light remembers, "The stage was extremely large and that may be one of the reasons why Kevin and Mira had difficulties. The stage seemed to swallow them up and they became very small."[20]

One day, tired of making an effort to understand the dialogue, Arthur Miller suddenly jumped off his chair and screamed: "What the hell is going on? I don't understand anything. I can't hear even one word of what you are saying."

Another afternoon during a dress rehearsal, Monty insulted all of the women in the cast, making it impossible to continue. Lehman Engel was called in to arbitrate the situation.

Monty as Constantine Treplieff in Chekhov's *The Sea Gull* at Phoenix Theatre in New York, 1954.

I took Monty by the arm and asked him to walk around the block with me. The essence of what I said after he expressed his unhappiness with the actresses was that he must have been aware of his feelings from the beginning, which was the only time he might have expressed himself so strongly and it was now too late; that the scheduled dress rehearsal had to be under way since the first preview was taking place a day later; and that under the circumstances I felt that [it was] Monty's responsibility to apologize and placate the actresses. Monty agreed.

A few days later he called me ... he was intensely unhappy but incapable of knowing why. He had a distinguished talent, a worshipful public and success nearly always. Whatever it was that bothered him, that drove him into a self-destructive way, I never knew.[21]

A few days before his return to the stage, Monty was interviewed on the radio by Mike Wallace for CBS's program *Stagestruck.*

MW: Monty, you are an actor of much demand. What makes you decide to leave the better paying of Hollywood or a possible Broadway production in order to come down to Second Avenue at the Phoenix Theater?

MC: I'm very lucky, I'm free. I do not have any commitment with several studios. I can do what I like! And Norris asked me "Would you like to do *The Sea Gull*?" Something that actually myself and several friends were working on, for some time. So they had the idea. We thought about it one night, we examined if we felt the same like two years ago and we said yes! That's all. We are all friends that includes Kevin McCarthy and Mira Rostova.

MW: How long has it been since you have done a play here in New York?

MC: I guess since '45, '46 — hmm '45.

MW: Do you like acting on stage?

MC: No. I do not like to act in any place but presuming [it] is my profession I'll act. No. I do not mean like that, but you achieve yourself down to a profession and it unqualifies you for other professions.

MW: Can you pick anything you'd rather do then?

MC: No. I'd rather be a bartender, but besides ... that....

MW: In as much as you have to act, why don't you act more on stage?

MC: Well it has to do with I guess only one thing, since I kept myself free, and the reason has only had to do with the material that comes my way.... I'm reading scripts, there is not a single one which has been offered to me or has been done, which I felt it should be done. So it has to do with the material.

MW: Rather than the media? You do not care where? Movies, television, radio.

MC: No not at all. Let's say that I like to do a television show with Frank Sinatra, if he comes up with a show and I'll be right for it, I'd do it in a second, and the same with the theater. Let's say that Arthur Miller writes a play where I would be right for it and he wants me for it, I'll do it in a second. I do not mean they must be that kind of playwrights, which are playwrights in a high-rise sense. If it interests me and I'm free to do it then I'll do it.

MW: It is a luxury, it is freedom, what you are talking about.

MC: It is also gambling. If you are not willing to take the gambling you do not have the luxury!

MW: Now, *The Sea Gull* will be finished at the Phoenix in the middle of June. What are your plans?

MC: I have no idea. There is a movie script that has been offered to me but I have not read it yet because I do not have time. Ten hours of rehearsal a day so I do not have any time to read the script, so I have to postpone until May 11th or May 12th. I'm gonna read the movie script.

MW: So good luck on May 11th. Thanks Montgomery Clift.
MC: Thank you.[22]

Tickets for the show quickly sold out, and all 1100 seats in the theater were occupied every night of the 5 weeks that the play ran. Everybody was curious to see a Hollywood star on stage.

The night of the premiere, the Phoenix Theater was packed with celebrities, from Marlon Brando to Marlene Dietrich, from Anthony Perkins to Harry Belafonte. Many others also came to applaud Monty's return with a production that had not been seen on stage for 16 years. Critics noticed a difference in the acting style of the performers. They praised the Hollywood star, but they slighted, as Monty predicted, Mira Rostova for her interpretation of Nina and felt she was handicapped by her thick Russian accent.

Monty took the bad reviews to heart and thought that the play was a total failure, especially for his own theatrical ambitions. Mira Rostova remembers, "I felt Monty was in the frame of mind like if he could choose he wouldn't do it."[23]

The Sea Gull closed after running for 5 weeks, one week earlier than originally planned. This was probably also due to Monty's disappointment and fatigue. This failure could be seen as the turning point of his artistic career. Subconsciously, the suffered disappointment would slowly push him to retreat into an alcoholic oblivion.

The Sea Gull was Monty's last performance on stage, despite the many offers he received in the following years. This included the part of Brick in the original production of the Tennessee Williams drama *Cat on a Hot Tin Roof,* which went to Ben Gazzara. In his last interview before his death, Monty said: "I love the stage but after a few months you can get tired. I would rather do three movies than play in one stage hit. I played in four flops in a row when I was about 17 and I was delighted. I was being paid to be trained."[24]

During that summer Monty resumed Dr. Silverberg's antidepression treatment, renting a cottage next door to his physician in Ogunquit, Maine. His presence in the little village aroused great curiosity, but this time Monty liked being the center of the attention. He attended all of the social events and held parties at his place, too. Ogunquit was a favorite gay resort and during a "queer" party, he did not miss the opportunity to get wildly drunk. When the owners of the cottage visited him, they found the house in terrible condition: the furniture was half destroyed, food and garbage was everywhere, and Monty was lying naked on the living room sofa submerged in empty bottles.

His agent kept sending him scripts that systematically ended up in

Monty relaxing on the beach reading a script, 1954.

the garbage without being read. The only exception was *The Execution of Private Slovik*, which interested him significantly because the main character was very similar to Prewitt in *From Here to Eternity*.

His financial situation was not very florid; he made unprofitable investments and he had to pay over half a million dollars in taxes. His debt increased and he owed $10,000 to his agent. He needed someone who could take care of his life, especially in the financial administration department.

His friend Harvey Orkin introduced him to Marge Stengel after his secretary Virginia McDowall, Roddy's sister, quit. "I will never forget my first meeting with Monty. I'd just walked into his house and he asked me if I wanted something to drink, but I was very shy and I refused. He excused himself for a moment and went to the kitchen to fix something to eat and then came back with a piece of raw meat, something like liver or chicken, that he started to bite. I thought that that job was something ridiculous and I told Harvey I was not the right person for that kind of work. He begged me to try at least for six months, because, according to him Monty and I were made for each other."[25]

Marge stayed by Monty's side for 7 years, as his secretary, confidante, friend and nurse. Like a good, reassuring angel, she would leave him alone only at night to go back to sleep in her little studio apartment in Tudor City. She would screen all of his phone calls and visitors, and would check his bills before paying them, since they were often inflated by ruthless salesmen looking to take advantage of his presumed richness. She learned to recognize which people were Monty's real friends like Roddy McDowall, Libby Holman and Elizabeth Taylor.

She never asked any questions or expressed any personal opinions regarding some of the strange habits that her employer had. She was always alert and ready to defend his privacy. "Once I entered his bedroom and I saw an open closet and I was very impressed that inside were hanging some women's clothes. I'm sure they belonged to him."[26]

Dr. Silverberg was the only person she felt very hostile toward. "Although Monty adored him and thought of him like a god, I could never forgive the way he answered me when I called him in an emergency because Monty had a fit for too much drinking. He told me to mind my own business! I've never dared to [say] anything because Monty worshipped him. Later I heard he was gay too and I think that secretly he was in love with his patient, something very possible because it would happen to everybody to fall for him."[27]

Nevertheless, Marge's presence was not enough to heal Monty's "*mal de vivre*" that possessed him and shaped his destiny. His friendship with the Greens and the McCarthys had cooled, and every new attempt to make his life happy and serene was sunk by his uncontrollable behavior. One evening at Taylor's apartment, Monty was drunk and got very angry because Elizabeth decided not to go out to dinner after a quarrel with her husband, Michael Wilding. Jeanne Green recalls: "So we just said let's fix dinner here" since Fred and I were good cooks. Michael said, "Go to the kitchen and help yourself with whatever is in the kitchen." All we could find was eggs and some mushrooms and we decided to make an omelet, and Monty was furious, enraged. "We are going out!" and Fred said, "No, we are not going out. We are gonna be here," and Monty finally said, "All right, but if we are going to eat here I'll make the eggs," and he took the eggs away from Fred and he started beating them and spitting in them over and over again, just spitting. I thought, "This is crazy! What are we doing here? What is this about?" So I said to Fred, "Let's get out of here! This is insane! This is no life! We can't be with him! It's not possible be with him!"[28]

Evenings at Monty's home were not considered by everybody to be a painful experience; indeed, especially occasional guests liked them because they were amused by his crazy behavior and by his unstable temper. Robert Thom remembers: "I was at Monty's home for dinner one night. The woman I was with at the time was a young actress [Janice Rule], well known for her beauty. She had had one enormous hit on Broadway, but that was several years past. She worked, but her career was in trouble.... As we were leaving, Monty took her face in both hands (what strange uncoordinated hands they were!) and with tears in his eyes, as if he were filled with pity, a doctor recognizing an incurable disease, said tenderly: 'I do not understand it ... how can you act ... when you don't have any feelings?' It was some time before we saw Monty again. He called and he called and he apologized and he apologized. I told him my exact feelings in words that I think are still unprintable."[29]

In *Answered Prayers* Truman Capote uses an extreme, fictional style to describe a typical evening at Monty's home. The actor drops a cigarette into his bowl of Senegalese soup, and then stares inertly into space as if he were acting the part of a traumatized soldier, while his guests (including an improbable Tallulah Bankhead) pretend not to notice.[30]

Libby Holman was the only one who seemed not to be concerned with Monty's health and with his bizarre behavior. That summer of 1954, she was singing torch songs in a New York nightclub, and a couple of months later she went with Monty to Cuba to celebrate her musical success. Their friendship was working because it was based on mutual freedom and thoughtlessness. On Christmas they gave each other some gold Zippo lighters as presents as substitutes for the ones they regularly lost. On one in particular, Libby engraved, "Go ahead and lose it."

Once back from the holiday, Monty was involved in a car accident with Libby's new Simca and was hospitalized for a few days. Libby's attorneys ensured that the accident was not disclosed to the press.

The two friends were inseparable; they would spend their afternoons listening to Ella Fitzgerald records and Frank Sinatra songs, particularly to their favorite "I've Got the World on a String." One day while visiting the Metropolitan Museum they were impressed by a project of a Japanese house. Monty wrote to the famous architect, Lewis Munford, for advise on how they could build a similar one for themselves.[31]

They were so notorious as a couple that in the summer of 1955 an off–Broadway theater production briefly staged a comedy based on their affair called *Single Man at a Party,* whose film rights were bought by Joan Crawford. Thornton Wilder was a habitué of Libby's home at Treetops, and he wanted Monty to appear in his new forthcoming production *The Alcestiad* (later called *Life in the Sun*) in Edinburgh. Monty asked the playwright to make some major changes to his part but Wilder refused and left so offended by the actor's request that he stopped talking to him. When Monty died in 1966, Isabel Wilder asked her brother if he minded her going to the funeral and if he wanted to join her: "Do you really want to go? That's so wonderful of you. I can't."[32]

Monty spent all of his time with Libby and lost interest in work. He was always insecure about the offers he received and always demanded new, impossible changes to the scripts he considered, losing a lot of opportunities like acting with Alec Guinness in *Sons and Lovers* based on the D.H. Lawrence novel.

Due to Elizabeth Taylor's interest and because of his increasing financial difficulties, Monty accepted the role of John Shawnessey in MGM's *Raintree County,* based on the best-selling, 1100 page novel by Ross Lockridge, who won an MGM contract which gave $150,000 to the author and film rights to the studio. But despite the novel's success, Lockridge killed himself soon after its publication.

The story took place in Indiana during the Civil War, and Monty played a young, idealistic school teacher, who married a neurotic "Southern belle" played by Taylor. Eva Marie Saint (winner of an Oscar for *On the Waterfront*) played the teacher's true love, who would be with him only at the end, after a mad Taylor tragically dies in the local swamps. MGM offered Monty a $300,000 salary, but he insisted on signing for $250,000, saying that the difference would be better used to improve the film.

Raintree County was filmed in Panavision, a revolutionary system with 70mm film that made color resolution brighter and more vivid. Edward Dmytryk, who had previously had a hit at the box office with the screen adaptation of another bestseller, Herman Wouk's *The Caine Mutiny*, was to direct the movie. The huge success made Hollywood forget his involvement with the "Red List" during the McCarthy era.

The shooting of the film started in Hollywood in March 1956. The production company found Monty a big house on exclusive Down Ridge Road, and provided him with a butler, a Filipino cook and a car with a chauffeur. The house was only twenty minutes away from Elizabeth Taylor's residence. *Raintree County*'s ambition, with a budget of about $6 million, was to reach the same fame and success as another "Southern" movie, *Gone with the Wind*, which had made the producer, Selznick, a fortune. The result, though, was only a modest imitation aggravated by too many allegories. One was Elizabeth Taylor's character's obsession with the possibility of having been born with black blood in her veins, representing the South's corruption and the ruining of the North, which was her dreamer and poetic husband.[33]

Raintree County's story took place over several decades and in the beginning Monty had to look like a 20-year-old boy with high hopes. He was very concerned with his look and asked the make-up artist to do as much as he could to make the wrinkles around his eyes disappear. Those eyes, which he considered his best asset, were so sensitive that he was often forced to use eyedrops because of the reflection from the lights and to wear prescription glasses off the set. The result was perfect. It was his first film in color and he looked more handsome than ever.

Between takes, Monty would spend time with Elizabeth and her husband, even though their marriage was on the rocks. He also became very good friends with screenwriter Millard Kaufman, becoming particularly attached to his 6-year-old daughter, Mary, often buying her presents and staying in touch with her until his death.

S I X

Tragic Destiny

"You bastards! If you dare take one photograph of him like this,
I'll never let another one of you near me again!"
— *Elizabeth Taylor*

On Saturday, May 12, 1956, Jack Larson spent the entire afternoon in Down Ridge at Monty's house, where the actor was resting, exhausted from work and from the endless quarrels between Elizabeth Taylor and her husband. In the past three years he had spent so much time with them that many thought they were having a ménage à trois. "I do not understand it," he confided to Billy LeMassena, "I love men in bed but I really love women."

That afternoon Elizabeth invited him to a dinner at her place. One of the guests was to be a priest, who loved Monty's interpretation in *I Confess* and who was very interested in meeting him. After refusing the invitation three times, Monty finally accepted so as not to disappoint Elizabeth, even though he was very tired, did not feel like going out and he had already given his driver the day off. The guests at the dinner party included Kevin McCarthy, who was in town filming *Invasion of the Body Snatchers*, Rock Hudson, a very close friend of Elizabeth's, with his new secretary-wife Phillys Gates and the Dmytryks. The priest ended up not showing.

That morning Monty had suffered from a strong hangover, so he decided not to drink too much. Indeed, he drank very little, surprising everybody and behaving in a very quiet manner. The evening was very relaxing, and they played Frank Sinatra records and listened to songs by

102

Nat King Cole. First to leave the party were the Dmytryks and Kevin McCarthy — McCarthy had to leave for San Francisco the next day. Monty told him to wait because he wanted to drive with someone in a car ahead of McCarthy's.

"It was about 11 o'clock," McCarthy remembered. At that time Beverly State Drive was not built up; it was a fairly lonely road and there were a couple of sharp turns in the hill going down. I became aware that Monty's car was coming up very close behind me, the headlights were much too close and I was getting a little bit nervous and there was a turn coming ... so I tried to pull away from his car by speeding up a little bit and I made the turn very quickly, but on the next turn I was watching in my rear mirror and suddenly there were no lights.... There was nothing there. I turned my car around and I drove back the 150–200 yards to the point that he seemed to be. My headlights disclosed that his car was smashed up, the front was all battered and bashed. I looked in and Monty's body was crunched underneath the dashboard somehow. I tried to open the door but I could not get it open to see ... as I looked in I could see what looked like his face all ripped apart, blood and no sound of any kind. I assumed, I guessed I was afraid that he was dead. There seemed that there was no alternative to leave him and drive back up to the house and alert Michael and Elizabeth."[1]

Taylor went on:

Suddenly Kevin came lurching, white faced, into the living room. He was saying something incoherent and finally one got the words, "My God, oh God, Monty's dead."

We all ran down. My only thought was to get into that car and Monty would be alive. The doors were jammed shut, but we could see that Monty's head looked like it had been smashed right into the steering wheel and the windshield. He was bleeding from the head so much that it looked like his face had been halved. Finally somebody got one of the doors open and we all kind of backed away from the car and then I crawled into the car and lifted him away from the steering wheel. I found that he was breathing and moaning. All my revulsion about blood absolutely left me. I held his head and he started coming to. You could hardly see his face. It was like pulp. He was suffering terribly from shock, but he was absolutely lucid. There was a tooth hanging on his lip by few shreds of flesh, and he asked me to pull it off because it was cutting his tongue.

We had to wait forty-five minutes for the ambulance. It got lost. The ambulance came and we got him out of the car and oh God, it was horrible. He was squirting blood all over his face. He never once complained. I rode in the ambulance, and by the time we reached the hospital his head was so swollen that it was almost as wide as his shoulders. His eyes by then

Monty's car after the accident in Bel Air, California, 12 May 1956.

had disappeared. His cheeks were level with his nose. The whole thing was
like a giant red soccer ball.

It wasn't till the doctors took him away that there was the shock of
finding myself covered with somebody else's blood. The sick, sweet smell
of it made me want to vomit. Later on I used to have nightmares about it
and remember his face.[2]

Reporters and photographers arrived on the site as quickly as the
ambulance; however, Monty's friends formed a human barricade to protect him. Elizabeth was so angry that she screamed, "You bastards! If you
dare take one photograph of him like this, I will never let another one of
you near me again!" There are no existing documents of that tragedy except
for a photograph of Monty's crushed car.

During the ride in the ambulance Monty joked with the nurses saying, "Gentlemen, let me introduce you to Elizabeth Taylor!"

Cedars of Lebanon Hospital doctors performed a very delicate and
difficult reconstructive surgery, without using any plastic surgery, despite
what the press often reported. The most difficult task was to reconstruct
his tooth because his upper jaw was completely crushed and it was wired
closed for three weeks. His nose was broken in two and his upper lip was
badly lacerated.

In 1962 during a television interview for the promotion of *Freud*,
Monty said: "When they showed me in the hospital a picture that was in

the paper of the car, I could not believe I was in the hospital bed. It was so demolished, and it was a result of just plain tiredness after shooting. I was so tired … to ride into a power pole. If the big box knocked down on me I would not be here to talk to you."[3]

Fatigue and sleepiness were not the only causes that provoked the accident. The mix of alcohol and drugs combined with perennial tension, made him drowsy and stupefied.

Monty endured his pain with dignity, and none of his friends remember him ever complaining during his convalescence at the hospital or at his home on Down Ridge Road. His father, Bill, visited him from New York, putting aside the personal tension they shared.

The main problem caused by the accident was the effect it had on *Raintree County*. Luckily producer Dore Schary had purchased an insurance policy to protect the entire cast against possible delays in the filming schedule. So the shooting was suspended until Monty fully recovered, and his hospitalization bills and the extra production costs were refunded by the insurance company. Such wide insurance coverage was a new thing for Hollywood, but from that moment on it became a usual procedure in the film industry.

After nine painful weeks of convalescence, Monty, with a wired jaw and with Elizabeth's support, decided to go back to work. Jack Larson remembers his friend, in a moment of weakness, crying in front of a mirror after looking at his face, afraid that he would never be the same again. His still slightly swollen face was not the same; it now looked fake, with a staring expression. His eyes, his best feature, were not always clear but kept their expressive fascination.[4] Although Dmytryk agreed to shoot him from his less damaged, right side, it did not work well. Monty still looked as if he had prematurely aged and like he had lost weight.

One night he suddenly disappeared; his telephone rang but there was no answer. Everybody looked for him in vain. Finally, Dmytryk and screenwriter Millard Kaufman went to his apartment and they found the door of his room open. Monty was asleep in bed, with his head not two feet from the telephone, dead to the world. He still clutched a cigarette in his hand: it had burned deep into the flesh of both his index and middle fingers and had finally gone out. The morning after this he arrived on the set dressed and groomed with Band-Aids covering his burns, ready to work as if nothing had happened.

To relieve some of the back and jaw pain caused by the accident, Monty was taking a lot of pills and he had started to inject codeine. Columnist Hedda Hopper caught him doing it in his trailer one afternoon, even though he claimed that it was only vitamins. His behavior soon went back to being strange and unpredictable. If his behavior during a dinner in a restaurant in Danville, Kentucky, with the state governor and his wife, was faultless, the night after, during another social event with Elizabeth, he cut and ate his blue-rare steak with his hands after coating it with a thick layer of butter and pepper. Another night he was found in a state of mental confusion while he was running naked through an upper-class residential area of town. After this episode, a policeman was put on his porch every night for the duration. The officer was quite won over by Monty's charm, and he would often have long conversations with him, while gently encouraging him to go back into the house and to bed.

When he was in a good mood, Monty would also play nasty jokes on the crew, faking that he was sick or hurt or staining his clothes with fake blood stolen from the make-up room. He enjoyed making everybody worry and then apologizing like a little child. *Raintree County*'s crew set some code words to be used when Monty was drunk or in a dark mood: bad was "Georgia," very bad was "Florida," and worst of all was "Zanzibar."

In his diaries, writer Christopher Isherwood remembers a dinner with the cast's dialect coach Marguerite Lamkin: "Clift behaved neither worse nor better than I'd expected. He arrived drunk, crumpled somewhat during supper, but he didn't spill anything and left soon after. I was really shocked by the change in his appearance since I saw him last. Nearly all of his good looks have gone. He has a ghostly shattered expression ... Monty is touching and very anxious to be friendly, but oh dear, how sorry he is for himself!"[5]

A lot of people did not recognize him or they could barely contain their astonishment when they noticed his dramatic changes. For a long time, Monty removed all the mirrors from his house and allowed only his closer friends, like Jack Larson, to visit him. A few weeks later, his face finally assumed a more natural expression.

Once the film was completed, he decided to stay in California longer to enjoy the good weather. His mood improved and in October, he gave a party to celebrate his 36th birthday and to thank all of his dearest friends. Dmytryk said that he enjoyed working with Monty, who was a "real genius," the "most creative actor" he had ever met.

Raintree County was released in an unorthodox way, as a traveling show. In fact, the film premiered in one city at a time. It had an intermission and a higher ticket price due to its 165-minute length. Audiences ran to see the film, mostly because they were curious to see Monty acting in some scenes with his "old face" and in others with his "new" one. *Raintree County* earned $6.5 million at the box office despite the generally bad reviews. Monty considered the film "a monumental bore."

Producer Dore Shary, Elizabeth Taylor, Monty and Eva Marie Saint on the MGM backlot during the filming of *Raintree County,* 1956.

His return to New York was still a shocking surprise for some of his friends, like Merv Griffin who remembers:

> The bell of my apartment rang late on a Wednesday night, and since the intercom wasn't working properly, I took my dog and went downstairs to see who it was. I opened the door a crack and saw an unfamiliar man, who wore an overcoat and a wide-brimmed hat. He was standing perfectly still, the hat covering his eyes.
>
> "What can I do for you?" The man did not say a word. "What do you want?"
>
> My heart started to pound and I was about to slam the door when the man whispered: "You don't know me, do you Merv?"
>
> I knew the voice instantly: "Monty ... I couldn't tell it was you. It is so dark out there."
>
> He turned and walked quickly away. I called after him but he kept walking. Kevin McCarthy later told me Monty had made a number of stops that night, and very few people had passed the test.[6]

Another night Monty was invited to be part of a reading that Norman
Mailer organized for his play based on *The Deer Park*. Among the guests
in attendance were Kevin McCarthy, Anne Bancroft and Gore Vidal. Adele,
Mailer's wife at the time, recalls:

> That evening we were waiting for Monty, the only one of the cast who had
> not yet arrived. The bell rang, and when I opened the door, he was there.
> I hope my face didn't show my shock. It was the first time I'd seen Monty
> since the accident....
>
> It was not the same beautiful face I had known. Badly damaged in the
> crackup, it looked made over, and in the procedure, the fine features had
> undergone a slight thickening. Under the circumstances, the doctors had
> done a superb job, creating a facsimile of Montgomery Clift. But the lumi-
> nosity, that special sensitivity in his face, was gone. He even talked oddly
> with certain stiffness in the way he moved his mouth.
>
> We were genuinely glad to see each other, though I knew him only slightly,
> and he gave me a warm hug. There was something so lost and fragile about
> this man that my heart went out on him. "Oh Monty, I'm so happy to see
> you." When he responded with a smile, I saw a glimpse of the face I had
> known. He was his sweet self that night, and it was one of the few times
> I'd seen him when he didn't get roaring drunk.[7]

One morning in November of that year, Billy Redfield showed up at
Monty's doorstep, informing him that Marlon Brando wanted to talk to
him in private. Ten minutes later, Brando knocked on the door. He was
wearing the costume and make up from the movie he was currently shooting, *The Teahouse of the August Moon,* for which he had to shave his eye-
brows. The two actors talked for several hours and Jack Larson, who was
there to take Monty to the orthopedist, watched them through the large
windows outside in the garden.

After Brando's departure, Larson drove Monty to the doctor's office.
In the car, Monty was still very moved. With tears in his eyes, he said that
Marlon had wanted to meet him to see how he was doing and that he had
sent Redfield before just to check and make sure that he was not drunk.[8]
Brando said that he had always admired him and that he had been root-
ing for him to win the Oscar for *A Place in the Sun* the same year he was
up with *A Streetcar Named Desire.*

A story circulated in Hollywood that Brando would always ask his
agent how much money Monty was making for his film and he would
always want an extra dollar. Brando also admitted that he had always been
jealous of him; always so envious that he would go to see his movies and
say: "How can he do that? How can he be that good?" Before leaving his
meeting with him he added: "You are what I challenge myself against. Take

care of yourself for me so I can keep challenging me because you are all I have."[9] Years later Marlon himself told the story to Maureen Stapleton, adding that he had begged Monty to join AA and even offered to go with him and help dry him out.

Monty's next film would have been *Moby Dick,* directed by John Houston, but the idea of playing a more interesting role, like the character Noah Ackerman in *The Young Lions,* made him change his mind about taking the part of Ishmael. As he later confessed to Charlton Heston: "I'm not certain it [Moby Dick] is going to be great."[10]

Since he had visited Israel in 1948, Monty had great respect for Jewish people, whose heroism and courage he greatly admired. Finally, he had the opportunity to show these feelings through his art. It was Dmytryk who believed that he would have been a perfect Noah. After he read the script, Monty sent a telegram to the director with just one word—"Yes."

Later, when he was invited to dinner at his parents' house, he did not miss his chance to tease his father, who was anti-Semitic, by telling him that he had been cast to play a Jew. "I was picked because I look so Jewish," he said. "Everybody thinks I'm Jewish."[11]

But it was his mother who got upset. "Monty dear, why are you doing this to me?" The tone of her question took Monty back to the times in his childhood that he had tried to be independent and make his own decisions but she would tell him that he was wrong. "Oh Ma! You are such a cunt, such a cunt!" He replied to her, exactly as he had in those times, and then he left.[12]

Sunny began calling her son every day, but Marge would tell her that Monty was not at home. The obstinate mother tried many times to act as nicely as possible with the secretary. One day she even sent her a curious present, a waste-paper basket. "I do not really know what she meant giving me that present, I was only respecting Monty's orders that he absolutely did not want to talk to her," she said.[13]

His decision to make *The Young Lions* was taken with great seriousness. He started to train himself for his character and he would often take long walks in Central Park with his script to learn his lines. This, along with his weekly sessions with Dr. Silverberg, were the only times that he would go outside. He preferred to invite friends like Greta Garbo over.

Monty became very fond of her, and developed a little crush on her. One night after he walked her home, he kissed her good night. "Her lips are chapped" was his only comment about it.

One afternoon Garbo met Salka Viertel and writer James Bridges at Monty's townhouse. She arrived with a bandanna on her head and dark sunglasses and went straight out into Monty's garden terrace. After drinks in the garden, Garbo followed Monty into the kitchen, where the two of them conversed over a tin of caviar. "Here are two of the most glamorous people in the world and what are they talking about?" Salka laughed. "The dishwasher they never used because they never entertain!"[14]

To get into his part the already slender Monty lost eleven pounds and he flattened his nose with putty and distended his ears. It was the first and last time on stage or in film that Monty used make-up devices as part of his interpretation.

His make-up was inspired by a photograph of Kafka, taken the year of his death, in which the writer looked almost skeletal, with frightened eyes and ears that stood out like a bat's. Monty had been observing that image since Thornton Wilder got his inspiration from Kafka for his unfinished play *The Emporium,* which was written for Monty.

SEVEN

Changes

"He's a crazy drunk, a pill head, confused quarrelsome."
— Joseph Mankiewicz

The Young Lions tells the story of three men whose lives are coincidentally intertwined: Noah Ackerman, a poor American Jew, Michael Whiteacre, an ambitious entertainer, and Christian Diestl, a Nazi officer. When Dmytryk told Monty that he was uncertain about whether to cast Tony Randall or Dean Martin for Michael's part, his reaction was one of disinterest. After he saw a movie with Randall later that same day, however, he called the director and said, "Take Dean Martin."[1]

Although Brando was under contract with 20th Century–Fox, he definitely wanted to appear in the film. He had his agent approach Dmytryk and tell him that Brando would make the picture on the condition that Christian's character was made more human. In response to this, the director had Brando's character die with his arms spread like those of Jesus when he was crucified.

Monty was furious that the script was changed to suit Brando's request. As someone in the production commented, "When Monty is in a film, nobody else plays Jesus Christ!" Dmytryk watched the strong competition between the two actors' different personalities with amused detachment. "Monty was an exceptionally bright young man who liked to pretend he wasn't," Dmytryk later said.[2]

The Young Lions began filming in Paris and the three stars stayed at the Hotel Raphael. Monty got along right away with Dean Martin, who nicknamed him "Spider" because of his uncoordinated gestures. Martin

On location in France with the crew of *The Young Lions,* 1958.

took care of him every time he was too drunk to take care of himself. "I would put him to bed because he was always on pills," Dean recalled.[3] And Monty coached Martin through their most dramatic scenes together, the same way he did with Sinatra in *From Here to Eternity.*

One evening Dmytryk took Marlon Brando, Maximilian Schell and Monty to dinner at a Middle Eastern restaurant on the Left Bank. At the table Brando was silent while he listened to Monty talking, obviously agitated. At one point, Brando interrupted the conversation and brought up a sore subject by suggesting that he go and see a psychiatrist. Later when Brando started speaking in French, Monty spoke to the waiter in grammatically perfect French, but with a strong American accent, imitating Brando out of spite. It was his way of saying, "I think you are pretty damned pretentious."[4] Two or three times Monty disappeared mysteriously, as he had so often in the past.

Dmytryk and cinematographer Joe MacDonald from *Raintree County,* found out that he possessed duplicate passports so he could travel without the press knowing. One time he vanished for more than three days and he was found by Fox representatives at a third-rate brothel in southern Italy, dead drunk.

Everybody knew about his sexual preferences; it was not a secret. In fact, he had a male lover with him on the set. According to cameraman Duke Calahan, Monty's homosexuality was tormenting him more than ever, while Dmytryk thought he was just plain sick. "The women on the film wanted to meet both Marlon and Monty, but about Monty they'd say, 'I can help him,' which was a great mistake. Nobody could help him."[5]

A couple of times Monty caught Brando lurking behind the camera, watching him while he was acting. "Tell Marlon he doesn't have to hide his face, when he's watching me act," said Monty, amused by his colleague's behavior. Later Monty commented to Jack Larson that Brando was using only one-tenth of his acting talent.[6]

Dmytryk had learned from the *Raintree County* experience that Monty was in better shape in the morning, so he made it possible for all of the takes with him to happen during that time of the day. Monty carried a thermos with him on the set which he told everybody contained "fruit juice," but it was a mixture of bourbon, Demerol and fruit juice. Although he was often drunk, nobody ever complained of being sexually harassed by him.

Dmytryk asked the director of the production, Ben Chapman, to ensure that Monty got to the set on time each morning. One day, when Monty was leaving his hotel, he saw Chapman waiting for him by his car. Monty kept going round in the revolving door until Chapman went to grab him. He was behaving as if he were high. Although it was only a joke, others witnessed the scene and new gossip started, causing the legend of Monty Clift's eccentricities to grow.[7]

Before leaving Paris, Monty received a letter from Vittorio De Sica, asking him to contact his friend Italian director Renato Castellani, who was interested in giving him a part in a film on Napoleon, costarring Gina Lollobrigida. But the project failed to be completed.[8]

The filming of *The Young Lions* resumed in Hollywood. Monty stayed in West Los Angeles at 701 Stone Canyon Road. One night a very strange episode occurred. He arrived like a fugitive at the famous Chateaux Marmont Hotel, where he requested a room on the sixth floor. From the moment he stepped inside the room, a "Do Not Disturb" sign was seen hanging from his door. He told reception he did not want to be disturbed by anyone, and above all, not by his mother. "If she … calls, tell her … I'm not … here."

The suite was off-limits for nearly a week. When a floor maid finally gained access to the room, she wasn't prepared for the sight that awaited her. He'd taken the bulbs out of every fixture except one, and that had a very dim light. The windows were closed tightly and the draperies were drawn. All of the mirrors had been hidden in a corner with their backs facing outward. It was difficult to walk because of all of the empty liquor bottles on the floor. On one occasion a house boy from the hotel found him barefooted, wrapped in a bathrobe and slumped outside of the penthouse, his face buried in his hands. He was pounding on the door hollering for Libby.[9]

Shooting ended in October 1957, and in an interview with *Newsweek* (his first one since the car accident), Monty said: "I always expect the worst when I go to see any performance of mine. But I'm genuinely proud of Noah, the character I played in *The Young Lions*. I've done some really good things in the picture ... I think I've erred less than I have in any of the other nine pictures I made. I feel a great affinity for the character — a shy, sensitive introspective man of the people. I'm 37 and Noah is 25 but our characters met in this movie. Strange, isn't it? It's impossible to explain but I couldn't have played Noah ten years ago."[10]

The sudden sad news of Michael Todd's plane crash affected Monty's tranquility. Elizabeth Taylor had recently married Todd, and Monty flew to Chicago to attend the funeral. At the service he was appalled by the frenzy of fans who invaded the cemetery in hysteria, just to catch a glimpse of the movie stars.

On April 2, 1958, Monty arrived at New York's Paramount Theater for the premier of *The Young Lions* in the company of Libby. The evening was organized to benefit the Actors Studio Fund. At the screening, during the very first scene in which Monty appeared a woman in the audience suddenly stood up and exclaimed, "Is that him?" before fainting. It seemed like a scoop organized for the press, but it didn't take attention away from the high, artistic quality of the picture and from the first rate performances.

Following the screening, there was a formal dinner at the Waldorf Astoria, attended by Hollywood stars like Paul Newman, Anne Bancroft, Geraldine Page, Marilyn Monroe and Don Murray with Hope Lange, who was Monty's wife in the film. After being complimented by every guest, Monty together with Libby, Hope Lange and Don Murray, waited for the reviews in the next day's newspapers.

They were a big disappointment. The *New York Times* critic Bosley Crowther wrote: "Mr. Clift is strangely hollow and lackluster as the sensitive Jew.... He acts throughout the picture as if he were in a glassy-eyed daze."[11] On the other hand, magazines like *Time* and *Newsweek* highly praised his interpretation, but it was not enough for Monty who complained to his friends by saying that he could have probably done much better.

In those days Monty made a new friend in popular stage and television comedienne Nancy Walker. She became very therapeutic for Monty, particularly because of her sense of humor and her sensitivity. "Nancy is so rich emotionally, she makes me feel rich."[12] They had casually met a couple of years before, when Monty went to see her in the show *Wonderful Town* and afterwards had dinner with her. Nancy's friendship was completely different from Monty's others. She refused to mother him or to treat him as an invalid. Marge Stengel remembers that when the two of them were going out together, she would refuse to check to see whether he was eating or not. "Isn't that what you are supposed to do when you go out to dinner?" Nancy used to say.[13]

The two friends became inseparable. They would call each other many times a day from wherever they were in the world, talking about everything and trying to have dinner together at least twice a week, even though Nancy was very busy taking care of her very ill husband at home. One day Monty took her to Buccellati, a famous Italian jewelry store, to choose a gift for Renée Zinnemann. They agreed on a beautiful string of pearls, but when they were out of the store, Monty gave the necklace to Nancy. "After all it's only a string of beads! ... It is something to celebrate my first year in analysis."[14]

Unlike Marge, Nancy did not worry about Monty's heavy drinking and his abuse of pills. It was her opinion that the real cause was the success which trapped him in the inescapable role of being both beautiful and damned. How Monty could get the prescriptions for all those pills was a mystery, because neither Rex Kennamer, his doctor in California, nor Arthur Ludwig, his physician in New York, would prescribe them to him. He was probably getting them through ruthless pharmacists, whose only interest was to extort money from him.

His health was weak; besides his physical pain he started to have frequent panic attacks. Often at night he would call the first friend to cross his mind, begging him or her to come over. One of them was Bill Gunn, a young black actor whom he had just recently met. At the time Gunn was working in Massachusetts, but one night he received a call from Monty who implored him to come back to New York immediately. Once he arrived at Monty's townhouse, nobody answered the intercom. Gunn knew that Monty would often pass out because of the pills and drinking, so he tried to call him from a public phone. After several attempts, Monty finally answered and candidly asked Gunn what he was doing in Manhattan at such a late hour.

In the fall, Monty agreed to accept half of his usual salary to star in *Lonelyhearts,* a film produced by Dore Schary (who had been the head of MGM and now was an independent producer) and directed by newcomer Vincent J. Donehue. Monty loved the moral integrity of his character and highly respected Schary, who had been part of the *Raintree County* production. Monty sent him a telegram saying, "Whenever you need me, just say 'show up.' At any stage, I'll be there."[15]

Lonelyhearts was a very loose adaptation of Nathanael West's best selling novel *Miss Lonelyhearts.* Monty played a newspaper columnist who wrote an advice-giving column. Robert Ryan and Myrna Loy played the newspaper editor and his wife, and Maureen Stapleton made her screen debut as a woman who constantly wrote to him.

As soon as Stapleton knew that Monty was part of the cast she called him. "Gee Monty, everything else is terrific, but that ending is so inappropriate. It's like taking Christ off the cross before he dies. I'm really disappointed." "Ha," laughed Monty. "This is Hollywood. I'm used to being disappointed."[16]

Filming lasted for 54 days without any particular problem other than a strange episode witnessed by United Press International reporter Vernon Scott and by Dore Schary. The two men invited Monty for a steak. While they were waiting for their New York steaks to be served, they could not help but notice the way people in the restaurant were observing and commenting on Monty's post-accident look. The actor became nervous and suddenly lost control; he grabbed a steak, coated it with butter, salt and pepper, and disappeared under the table. When Scott and Schary moved the table cloth, they saw him sitting with the piece of steak on his head, his hair covered with oil, howling with mad eyes and yelping like a suffering dog. "He looked like a frightened animal," remembered Scott.[17]

Donehue quickly understood Monty's weaknesses and tried to adapt the shooting schedule to the actor's demands, especially bearing in mind the fatigue that would hit him in the afternoon.

Maureen Stapleton gives a very poignant profile of Monty on the set. "We were sitting in my dressing room waiting for our call and he was lying with his head on my lap. He had always suffered from insomnia, now it was worse. I looked down and found he had fallen asleep, and I began to cry as I looked at his child figure before me and I just held him there until he woke up."[18]

Also Myrna Loy remembers him with moving words:

> Monty was a great talent…. He had extraordinary instincts. I had a scene with Bob Ryan that didn't work — it was beautifully written; there was just

too much of it. I brought it to Monty's dressing room, where we often lunched together. "Something's wrong with this scene," I told him. "It won't play this way." He took a pencil and just starting striking out words, like a surgeon removing his hundredth appendix. His cutting saved that scene and strengthened my impact. His observations about the script were always astute and correct. He would have made a great director, which eventually he wanted to be. "Would you ever direct yourself?" I asked him. "Are you kidding?" he replied. "As a director, I simply wouldn't put up with all the crap from me."[19]

Many spoke about a romance between Loy and him, especially about the big crush the actress had on Monty, but she completely denied the innuendo in her autobiography, stating that she just mothered him. She only felt the desire to protect him and tried to help him to overcome his shyness. She thought that most of Monty's problems were imaginary and related to his denial of his homosexuality.

Robert Ryan's opinion was much harsher. "Monty was very ill, extremely ill, looking almost like a dying man. There was something terrible in him. I never knew what tortured him, but he could not work in the morning and I did not know what he was doing. He just tormented himself, it was already a dead man, a dead man in waiting…. About the film? We had a terrible script but a great director."[20]

Robert Thom was often on the set, and he compared those six months spent in Monty's company to an intensive course on nursing, on becoming a bodyguard and on being a friend.

Some Like It Hot, Billy Wilder's comedy, was filmed at the same time as *Lonelyhearts,* but in another part of Goldwyn's studios. Monty always wanted to meet Marilyn Monroe and asked Dr. Kennamer, who had known her for years, to organize a dinner with her. It was a strange evening. Marilyn could not talk to Monty nor he to her, so at one point he took a walk with her. They soon broke through this barrier, and they started visiting each other's dressing rooms on the set during breaks, kissing and hugging as if they were old friends.

Once *Lonelyhearts* was completed, Dore Schary gave him a beautiful copy of the script bound in red calf leather and engraved with Monty's name and with the dedication: "To Monty. Thanks my friend. Dore." The gift moved him profoundly.

The film was a big flop at the box office and received terrible reviews, too. The only achievement was an Academy Award nomination for Maureen Stapleton, who was beaten by Shelley Winters for her role in *The Diary of Anne Frank.*

Back in New York, Monty's personal cook Elizabeth Guenster introduced him to graphology. Monty was so into it, that he would analyze the writing of every friend who was visiting him, giving his personal interpretation of their personality.[21]

At that time Monty started a relationship with Claude Perrin, a young Frenchman he had met just before filming *The Young Lions.* Perrin arrived in New York with the intention of working in the fashion industry, and for few years he worked as the assistant (and lover) of a fur maker, who tried to launch him as a designer with little success. Claude fell in love with Monty, fascinated by the glamour that surrounds a Hollywood movie star. He would write long love letters to Monty and personally deliver them to his house.

Perrin left his work and was supported by Monty, becoming more demanding every day and often stealing silver objects from Monty's house. The actor would always forgive him, and at the end of 1958 Perrin moved in with Monty permanently and served as his personal assistant. The relationship was a disaster because the Frenchman encouraged all of Monty's vices.

Monty's health was still very frail, and he suffered an increasing loss of memory and lucidity. Donald Windham remembers the night he received a call from Monty, who wanted to invite him to a private screening of *Lonelyhearts.* The writer was impressed with his "voice from the grave." Long silences were followed by slurred articulation, as he struggled to begin each word. Hours later Monty called back, perfectly natural, repeating the exact same conversation without remembering the previous one.[22]

On the professional side, Monty was no longer in great demand. Scripts that interested him were also very rare because his reputation for being a difficult actor to work with now preceded him. "Only a fool would hire Montgomery Clift," MGM producer Pandro S. Berman told Robert Thom, who suggested that Monty play Dimitri in Richard Brooks' film *The Brothers Karamazov.* Meantime, Monty refused all of the television offers that he received with contempt. "I'd rather put my energy into something that lasts more than just one night."[23]

In December of 1959 he finally received an interesting part, thanks to Elizabeth Taylor's intervention. Taylor was now free from her exclusive contract with MGM, and she was able to choose scripts she liked, achieving the same power Monty had had at the beginning of his acting career. Someone proposed that she play in an adaptation of Tennessee Williams' play *Suddenly Last Summer,* under the direction of Joseph Mankiewicz. The original play was part of a project called *The Garden District,* a presentation of two one-act plays, whose first part *Something Unspoken* was removed, creating some difficulties in the adapted screenplay. At that time Williams was at the top of his fame. He had just received enormous success with the film version of *Cat on a Hot Tin Roof,* a film based on one of his plays.

Sam Spiegel had purchased the film rights of *Suddenly Last Summer* from Williams for $50,000. The producer was convinced that the movie would be as big a hit as *Cat on a Hot Tin Roof,* especially if he used a cast that included stars like Katharine Hepburn and Mercedes McCambridge, and if the screenplay was adapted by Gore Vidal (whose references to the sexual psychology of the characters struck Monty).

Although the film was set in New Orleans, *Suddenly Last Summer* was made at London's Shepperton Studios. The director and principal cast members were American, but British technicians were used and they were paid less than those in Hollywood and were as professional as their American colleagues. Monty landed at Heathrow airport accompanied by Marge. There he was welcomed by a group of reporters and photographers. His mood was not at its best and his health was still so bad that it had been very hard to find a physician willing to release a certificate of good health, as requested by the insurance company. Sam Spiegel, though, hoped he could find a doctor in England who could help him.

Marge had been by his side on two other movie sets, but she had never had a feeling that something terrible could happen to his health like she did this time. "The night before leaving for London I couldn't sleep. I thought how dangerous that trip would be. I wanted to protect him and so I decided to leave just to be close to him all the time."[24]

They stayed at the Savoy Hotel in two separate rooms. Marge kept being a secretary-angel, screening all of his phone calls and visits. But she could not control him 24 hours a day, especially on the set, which was strictly closed to visitors, or at night when she would return to her room.

Trouble would always arrive when she was not with him. At night in the company of Maurice Leonard, the 20-year-old receptionist of the Savoy, Monty would often get drunk and sexually wild. Later, Leonard wrote in a book about how easily he won over Monty's attention, quickly becoming the actor's favorite "sexual sport" in London.[25]

The atmosphere on the set was extremely tense as Mercedes McCambridge recalls. "Everybody connected with the movie was so unhappy. The ambience and the vibrations were upsetting.... I was bitterly unhappy, Elizabeth (just married again for the fourth time to Eddie Fisher) was still mourning Mike Todd. Miss Hepburn was suffering through Spencer Tracy's illness.... Joe [Mankiewicz] had something wrong with his hands ... a skin disease ... and he had to wear gloves all the way through the picture.... And of course Monty was in torment."[26]

During the early days of filming, Monty personally wanted to be sure of the director's good health. Mankiewicz appreciated Monty's worries and invited him to dinner. It was a big mistake because he in effect aided and abetted a delirious Monty, who was an unexpected surprise for someone not used to his bizarre behavior. According to the director, Monty was "a crazy drunk, a pill head, confused quarrelsome … no longer a hot property, simply a bad risk.'"[27]

After seeing some early rushes, Mankiewicz was ready to replace him. "Over my dead body" was Elizabeth's reaction, while Monty was completely impassive as he was stupefied by alcohol. As producer Sam Spiegel recalls, "We were frequently tempted to fire him, because it became increasingly difficult to work with him [but] I was very fond of him. I spent hours and hours practically nursing him, postponing shooting until I knew he was calm and we'd given him enough coffee and counter medicines to counteract whatever drugs he was taking."[28]

The hot humid weather made filming more difficult for the cast and particularly for Monty. All the scenes were cut in small takes. One was even cut into 14 parts, sometimes containing merely one line per part. Taylor and Hepburn always stayed very calm. Daily, Elizabeth would push him to give his best, while Katharine would never get tired of rehearsing extra times with him in the same way that she used to cope with Spencer Tracy's alcohol problems.

The irony of this was that Katharine Hepburn was known to be intolerant of male homosexuals (she was apparently unaware of Monty's homosexuality) and she disliked the part she had in the film as the mother of a gay man, because it was full of morbid, sexual overtones. Supposedly, Spencer Tracy had to explain to her in laborious detail what kind of sexual activities two men engaged in. Hepburn's incredible patience was quickly exhausted after spending one weekend trying to dry Monty out. "None of my arguments did any good. I thought he was weak. Simpatico but weak."[29]

Every morning a Rolls Royce driven by chauffeur Ray Price would take Mercedes McCambridge and Monty to the Shepperton Studios. En route to the set, the car would pass by Wormwood Scrubs prison. McCambridge later wrote:

> We just sat in the back seat of the Rolls Royce and looked out at the hulking grey stone hell. Monty swore a lot in his everyday conversation, but from his sore, swollen mouth on the Wormwood Scrubs mornings his profanities had a terrifying obscenity. It is my most vivid memory of Monty Clift. Milky-eyed, sweating from all his pores, the sweetly-sickly odor of vodka, fetid and foul. He was haggard; the once so-beautiful face scarred and hollowed into deep grooves where the stubble of beard grew already

grey. Through the closed windows of the Rolls, he shouted fiercely at the wet fortress of Wormwood Scrubs. He called to the "poor locked-in bastards, sons of bloody bitches!" He wanted them to know that he belonged in there with them ... that the real criminals are on the outside ... that the insane ones are not in the crazy houses. Monty had a cackle laugh, flat and cruel when he wanted it to be. As the driver pulled away from the ugly façade of Wormwood Scrubs, Monty's snide, giddy giggles would diminish until his head fell back into a heavy drugged sleep ... on his way to his day's work![30]

Monty would often visit Elizabeth at her suite at the Dorchester Hotel; he would sit on the couch for hours or balance precariously on the railing of the balcony with a drink in his hand just staring into space, as Eddy Fisher recalled in his autobiography. "I felt very sorry for him, but Elizabeth didn't seem to pay too much attention to the way he was. She accepted it, and maybe even understood there was nothing she or anyone else could do to prevent him from destroying himself!"[31]

One night Monty made a spectacle of himself yet again. After getting roaring drunk he passed out in the famous Stork Room bar and he had to be carried out on a stretcher when they couldn't bring him round. Two waiters helped him into a taxi, and he bellowed old sailor songs as the cab pulled away.[32]

In a "restless" interview with the British newspaper the *Sunday Express*, after just completing the film, Monty wept, lay on the floor and swore while answering Roderick Mann's questions. He expressed his complete dissatisfaction with the part he played and his disappointment with Tennessee Williams' disinterest in discussing the role with him. "Tennessee doesn't give a damn — as long as he gets his film rights. I never even met him, [and] James Jones cared. So I went to see him."[33]

When the picture was finished something unpleasant happened. When Mankiewicz had called the final "cut" on the film, Katharine Hepburn strode across the stage to him.

"Are you absolutely sure you won't need my services anymore?" she asked.

"Yes I'm sure."

"Absolutely?"

"Absolutely."

Then in front of the shocked company, she leaned forward, spat straight into his eye, turned on her heels and marched directly into producer Sam Spiegel's office, where she gave a repeat performance.

"When I disapprove of something, it's the only thing I can think of to do. It's a rather rude gesture, but at least it's clear what you mean!"

Years later, Hepburn confessed that her act had not been prompted by her compassion for Monty, as many had thought, but that she spat at them for the way they had treated her.[34]

Suddenly Last Summer's publicity campaign was based completely around Elizabeth Taylor. This included a lurid poster of her wearing a white swimsuit and the words, "Suddenly last summer, Cathy knew she was being used for evil."[35]

The film was an unexpected success, earning $6.4 million despite the controversial plot elements involving homosexuality, cannibalism and incest. Strangely, the censors did not react to the movie, because they were satisfied with the chaste dialogues. Monty's interpretation received mixed reviews, probably because the film's overtones were not deeply understood. At the time even Tennessee Williams praised the film, but years later in his memoirs he expressed doubts about it, especially regarding Mankiewicz's depiction, which he considered too realistic, and Monty's unconvincing interpretation.

Once back in New York, although in better health, Monty ended up in the newspaper again. On the evening of September 24, 1959, Libby Holman saw fire engines outside Monty's townhouse and she forced her way through the crowd going inside while smoke from a fire was billowing out everywhere. She found Monty in bed with Claude, totally unaware of the danger. Workmen had accidentally left some flammable material in the lobby of his brownstone. For the first time in the news there was a reference to Montgomery Clift's ambiguous private life. The fire caused considerable damage, leaving the townhouse in terrible condition, but he refused to move to a hotel. With days of Marge's help, he cleaned up the house, because it was the only place where he felt secure.

Two months later, Monty was back to work on the set of 20th Century–Fox's *Wild River*, directed by Elia Kazan. The picture was filmed on location in Tennessee, in the area around Chickamauga Lake and the city of Cleveland. Bill Clift was originally from that region, and one day some of Clift's relatives from Chattanooga showed up on the set with a big fruit basket, excited to meet with Monty. He refused to see them and locked himself up in his hotel bathroom in Cleveland until they were gone.

This time, Monty left both Marge and Claude at home; they were both "punished" after a quarrel. A young, beautiful actress Donna Carnegie, who like Marge became a shadow that followed him everywhere, accompanied him.

Marlon Brando was Elia Kazan's first choice, but the actor was unavailable. So, the director was convinced by an executive producer, Spyros Skouras, who suggested Monty. Kazan, who had directed him 17 years earlier in *The Skin of Our Teeth* was not sure about casting him. Only when Monty promised to stay away from alcohol, did the director decide to take a chance and work with him again. Kazan remembers: "The worst problem I had with Monty was his dramatic coach, Mira Rostova ... [she] appeared on my set the first morning and took a stand behind the camera. 'Aha' I said to myself, 'I have a co director.' I couldn't check on what signals of approval or disapproval she was conveying to my hero, but I knew that a glance at the wrong time could make trouble for me so, I told Monty I didn't want her to be there and she disappeared.... When she'd been excluded from my set, she continued, I'm sure to work with Monty at night.

Monty as Chuck Glover in Elia Kazan's *Wild River,* 1959.

At least she kept him distracted until dawn, so I never inquired into what they did between.... He always showed up in the morning, quivering but ready and willing, and perhaps I have her to thank."[36]

Monty played government agent Chuck Glover, who is sent from Washington to convince an old, fierce woman, played by Jo Van Fleet, to leave her island in the middle of a river before it is flooded by a new dam. Glover falls in love with the old woman's niece, played by Lee Remick.

Remick was fascinated with Monty's kindness and vulnerability. She established a maternal relationship with him. "His body was bird-like. He was very thin and all bones.... He was clearly a troubled soul. His lack of self-esteem even with his friends, although he had many, made me feel very moved, touched and sad."[37]

Lee Remick was a young mother of two children, and although she was only 24 years old, she was very tenacious and mature. Monty felt very close to her and received comfort from her and gave comfort to her in particular when her husband, producer and director William Colleran, was involved in a terrible car accident. "I was absolutely crushed and destroyed, but he was just like a rock by my side."[38]

Twentieth Century–Fox did little to promote *Wild River,* and the film was quickly pulled from theaters before it had a chance to take hold, despite good reviews. In Europe the picture was highly acclaimed by audiences,

With Lee Remick in a scene from *Wild River*, 1959.

who gave the credit to Kazan. He fought for a better American distributor for what he called "one of his favorites."[39]

Wild River was also a favorite of some French film critics, like director François Truffaut, who considered it a masterpiece, and prestigious magazines like *Cahiers du Cinéma* which named it one of the 20 best films ever made. The most appreciated compliment came from Arthur Miller, who wrote a letter to Monty in which he sincerely recognized and praised him.

At the beginning of 1960 Monty received a notification of eviction from the owners of his townhouse, which was in need of major work after the fire incident. By a stroke of luck Monty found a bigger townhouse for sale, with four floors, seven bedrooms, six fireplaces, six bathrooms, a 600 square foot living room and a garden only three doors down from his place. His new address became 217 East 61st Street.

Serge Obolensky, the owner of the townhouse, told him that that house had been a wedding gift from President Theodore Roosevelt to Alice Longworth. Monty was very impressed, and after he moved in at the end of January, he spent six months trying to furnish it, but the space was so big that many rooms stayed unfurnished for a long time. Monty preferred very simple and classic styles, painting the walls a light shade of beige; the only contrast of luxury was a collection of silver objects exposed in the living room. "I don't like a place all cluttered up with stuff. Whatever I have here was brought piece by piece, as I saw something I could enjoy living with."[40]

Monty loved his new home, but the problems connected to the moving disoriented him. Claude's daily presence would create violent arguments with Marge, who was sure that his lover negatively influenced Monty's hysterical and irritable behavior. So after seven years of loving care and maternal assistance, Marge decided to leave him. She was convinced that Monty's constant demand for help would soon take over her life, too. "It was between my life and his life. I had to leave before it was too late."[41]

EIGHT

John Huston

"What are you going to do … kill me?"
"I'm seriously considering it!"
— John Huston

In the spring of 1960, Monty was suffering from a variety of illnesses. He would often lose his balance and memory and his sight also worsened. Dr. Ludwig diagnosed premature cataracts in his eyes and discovered a form of hypoparathyroidism, a condition that prevented his glands from producing enough calcium, resulting in terrible cramps and spasms. He was hospitalized for ten days at Mount Sinai Hospital for alcoholic hepatitis. Before checking into the hospital, he had signed a contract to play a major role in Arthur Miller's *The Misfits*, directed by John Huston. "I've decided to do *The Misfits* because I don't appear until page 59," he joked. "I only read ten pages of my part and I called Arthur and said I would do it."[1]

"He was so pleased to be working with me and Huston and Marilyn on this film that I couldn't believe he would betray his responsibility," recalls Miller in his autobiography. "Indeed he never missed an hour's work: he had his entire part memorized before shooting began and was always on time despite the long delays in filming the picture."[2]

Monty left for Reno alone, without Mira, Marge or Claude. Because he was an insomniac and afraid of not being able to sleep comfortably, he had his own bed shipped from New York to the Mapes Hotel in Reno, Nevada. He also asked for special thick, black curtains to be installed in his room so that he could be completely isolated in his bedroom. It was not enough, and he often spent long sleepless nights talking on the phone.

Monty studied his cowboy part with great enthusiasm. He practiced rodeo riding with wild horses and bulls. He cut his nose badly while helping a rider straddle a bull. The cut fit his role and was included in the script. The production had many problems with the insurance company because it refused to insure him, only eventually offering to cover him after the insistence of Miller and Huston.

The Misfits was based on real events. Miller had spent several weeks in Nevada obtaining a divorce from his first wife; there he met three cowboys who made their living selling wild horses. This inspired him to write a short story published in *Esquire* in October 1957. Later he adapted it as a screenplay, placing more emphasis on the character of Rosalyn Taber, played by Monroe, rather than on the three cowboys played by Clark Gable, Eli Wallach and Monty.

Monty played his part with extreme professionalism. In his first scene, during a telephone conversation with his mother, he tells her about a rodeo accident in which, miraculously, he escaped death and had his face covered with scars. Screenwriter Robert Thom in an article in *Esquire* openly accused Miller of having deliberately written those lines, knowing very well that Monty was a mother's boy and that his face had been smashed in an accident.[3] But Monty ignored those insinuations, even though they were probably not totally groundless because the script had not been completed by the time he was cast.

His excitement was not enough to make him stay away from abusing alcohol or drugs. Thanks to producer and "guardian angel" Frank Taylor, he was saved from a fight in a bar and from sleepwalking naked in the hotel's corridors.

Marilyn was indeed the one causing a lot of problems to the production, as John Huston ironically said: "She was taking pills to sleep and pills to wake up in the morning."[4] Monty and Marilyn shared an immediate feeling of closeness and mutual reassurance. "The only real trouble was when Marilyn was really sick and we had to suspend the production. As for lateness, we adjusted to it. I can sympathize with it. I know how a person feels when facing a big scene. You can get so worked up over it that you become physically sick. I think that was the case with Marilyn ... I must say that Huston never once gave any evidence of impatience. Whether this was due to his own serenity or whether he reasoned that things might get worse if he did blow up, I don't know."[5]

For her part, Marilyn commented that she was never romantically attracted to him, explaining that they were too much alike. "Two crazy people together.... Monty the misfit. Marilyn the misfit.... I look at him and I see the brother I never had and feel braver and get protective."[6]

With Arthur Miller in Nevada on the set of John Huston's *The Misfits,* 1960.

Together they looked like two babes in the woods, or two orphans in the storm. Monty was unable to completely accept himself because of his homosexuality and he was frustrated by the impossibility of expressing himself in his professional roles. On the other hand, Marilyn was trapped by a spontaneous superficiality that made her appear like a mere sex symbol or an object of desire.

Monty commented: "I have the same problem as Marilyn. We attract people the way honey does bees, but they are generally the wrong kind of people. People who want something from us, if only our energy. We need a period of being alone to become ourselves. To be an actor, you can't afford defenses, a thick skin. You've got to be open, and people can hurt you easily."[7] And Marilyn commented: "People who aren't fit to open the door for him sneer at his homosexuality. What do they know about it?"[8]

Monty spent lots of time in Monroe's dressing room, teaching her how to better act in her role. It did not take long for tabloids to write about an improbable romance between the two stars. Elizabeth Taylor was said to be furious when she heard the gossip. Taylor detested Marilyn, and according to Norman Mailer's biography of Monroe, Eli Wallach, who witnessed a meeting between Elizabeth and Marilyn in the Polo Lounge in Beverly Hills, stated that Taylor said, "Get that dyke away from me." When Taylor heard that Mailer was going to use the quote, her lawyers threatened to sue the writer for $6 million, but Mailer got some witnesses to confirm what she had said and so no legal action was taken.[9]

Libby Holman visited Monty on the set for a weekend. They had not seen each other since the fire in Monty's townhouse. Libby had just gotten married to homophobic painter Luis Schanker, who later forbade her to meet Monty again. It was the last time that they saw each other. During the filming of *The Misfits*, Monty again met Kevin McCarthy, though their friendship had ended years before. Huston had cast him in the little part of the husband who Marilyn was divorcing. The director had a meeting with Gable, Monty and him, but they only discussed acting techniques. The old intimacy between them was gone, and after the movie was finished they never saw each other again.

Monty's relationship with Clark Gable was very similar to the one he had had with John Wayne while filming *Red River*. Gable treated Marty and Marilyn like two stupid, little children. One afternoon they were all shooting a difficult scene in the desert. Gable got very upset because Monty lit a cigarette while he said a key line. Gable continued his speech until the take was over, but once he was back in his dressing room he exclaimed, "That goddamn fag stole the scene from me lighting that cigarette!" Frank Taylor tried to defend Monty saying that it was not Monty's style to do such a strange thing. The following morning Gable took a look at the rush and admitted he was wrong. "That faggot is a hell of an actor."[10]

In another scene they had together Monty, as written in the script, punched Gable's arm. In the next take, Monty, forgetting his colleague had arthritis, hit him again and Gable roared: "For Christ's sake cut that out. If you do that again, you little bastard, I'm going to land one on you!" Monty burst into tears and Gable turned incredulously to writer Michael Munn, who was on the set. "What the fuck is the world coming to?" he asked.[11]

Gable died of a heart attack twelve days after the completion of the film. A couple of days before, Monty had celebrated his 40th birthday at a party given by Huston, at which he behaved impeccably.

The making of *The Misfits* ended $500,000 over budget and 45 days later than the scheduled date, mostly due to Marilyn's lateness. Before returning to New York, Monty spent a few days in Los Angeles at the Bel Air Hotel, where he commented to the press that his next goal was to direct his own film. He also complained that, as an actor, he had always been judged and cast on the basis of stereotypes that were the exact opposite of who he actually was.[12]

On January 31, 1961, the cast of *The Misfits* attended the New York premiere at the Capitol Theatre. Monty arrived with Marilyn and they posed for the photographers. Even though she had just divorced Miller the previous week, for the sake of the film they pretended to be on good terms.

The picture was not a success. Audiences were puzzled by the deep psychology of the characters and by the complicated plot. Critical response was enthusiastic. *Newsweek* wrote, "[*The Misfits*] is superbly played by a fine cast,"[13] and the *New York Herald Tribune* added, "Can anyone deny that in this film these performers are at their best? You forget they are performing and feel that they are...."[14]

During a short vacation in Puerto Rico with his lover Claude, Monty learned from his agent that producer and director Stanley Kramer was interested in him for a role in his next production, *Judgment at Nuremberg*. The film was based on Abby Mann's teleplay, which had been broadcast by CBS-TV two years earlier. It was about the trial of Nazi war criminals held in 1948 in Nuremberg. According to Kramer, United Artists would finance the picture only if it had an all-star cast, so he chose Spencer Tracy, Maximilian Schell, Marlene Dietrich, Burt Lancaster (substitute for Laurence Olivier, who turned down the part at the last moment), Richard Widmark, and Judy Garland in a cameo.

When the director met with Monty at his brownstone, he was appalled by the brutal way the actor looked, "as if he had one foot in the grave,"[15] compared to the way he remembered him. Originally Kramer had the intention of casting him in the role of Colonel Lawson, but after reading the script, Monty found the character of Jewish Rudolph Petersen, who was sterilized by the Nazis because he was considered mentally challenged, to be more interesting. "I felt the original part they wanted me to play — the American prosecuting attorney — was wrong for me, but I was tremendously intrigued by a smaller role which obviously doesn't deserve my usual salary ... since it is only one scene and could be filmed in a single day.... I felt it was more practical to do it for nothing than to reduce my price or to refuse a role I wanted to play."[16]

Monty's usual salary of $200,000, which Kramer offered to pay him for the role of the prosecutor, was reduced to $50,000 for Rudolph Petersen (who originally had two scenes before being cut in the editing room). But Monty surprised the production by maintaining his position and refusing any fee, asking only for trip, board and lodging expenses. He wanted to teach MCA a lesson. In fact, he was resentful of his agency that did not take care of his professional interests in the past, because of his health problems. At the end of filming he almost sent them a near-empty envelope containing only the note, "Inside you'll find your percentage."

His part required 10 days of work at Universal Studios in Hollywood. Monty stayed at the Bel Air Hotel with Claude for three weeks where the final bill totaled $15,000. Shooting was harder than expected because Monty always went in front of the camera drunk and unable to remember his exact lines. He often apologized to the crew, but after the umpteenth attempt Kramer yelled at him: "Just forget the damn lines, Monty. Let's say you are on the witness stand, the prosecutor says something to you, then the defense attorney bitterly attacks you, and you have to reach for a word in the script.... Go ahead and reach for it. Whatever the word may be, it doesn't really matter. Just turn to Tracy on the bench whenever you feel the need and ad lib something. It will be all right because it will convey the confusion in your character's mind."[17]

Spencer Tracy, who had his own alcohol problems, grabbed Monty by the shoulders saying, "You are the greatest young actor alive. Look, it doesn't matter to Stanley or to me what the words are. Stop trying to remember the lines, and just look into my eyes and tell me how you feel."[18]

Monty took a picture of his mother out of his pocket and improvised the entire scene. It was one of the most powerful moments in a film that earned him his fourth Academy Award nomination, this time for best supporting actor.

Kramer adds: "Everyone felt compassion for Monty and got along well with him, but I think Monty and Judy [Garland] understood each other best. Both of their careers had reached a low point, and they were each struggling to find their way back. They both had incredible problems and in this there was obvious camaraderie."[19]

Monty's segment was finished by the time Garland's began, but he hung around the set, watching everything that was going on. When Judy did her scene, she was overweight and not as attractive as she used to be, but it helped her to be more like her German housewife character. Monty watched her, sitting in a corner with tears pouring down his cheeks, his jacket and shirt drenched. At the end of the scene, he made his way to where Kramer stood and still sobbing, mumbled, "She played that all wrong."[20]

During his California stay, Monty occasionally went out with Marlene Dietrich, whom he had met years earlier in Las Vegas at a Tallulah Bankhead concert during a break from *I Confess*. Dietrich once said that she always felt like she was capable of anything. If she had to swim across the Atlantic with a child, she could do it. But, she added, although she liked Monty, she couldn't help him.[21]

Once back in New York, he received an offer to appear on stage in an Actors Studio Production of James Baldwin's *Giovanni's Room*. Monty enjoyed the novel a lot but he turned down the offer because he not only thought he could not memorize the lines but he also felt uncomfortable playing the role of a homosexual. Moreover, by this time Monty was worried about the increasing problems he was having with his sight. The sunlight constantly bothered him and it often forced him to wear big, dark sunglasses.

He did accept John Huston's offer to star in a biographical film on Sigmund Freud. This would have been his big opportunity to again prove himself as the great actor he had always been, playing a character he finally felt was congenial to himself. Therefore, he refused Italian director Mauro Bolognini's proposal to shoot *Senilità* based on Italo Svevo's novel.

From the very beginning Huston had Monty in mind as the only possible actor to play such a complex and intense character as the father of psychoanalysis. Huston previously had made *Let There Be Light,* a short documentary on hypnosis as a treatment for battling fatigue. Eli Wallach had tried very hard to obtain the part of Freud. He dressed up in 19th century clothes to show Huston how much he resembled the real Freud. Nevertheless, the director needed a face that could speak and express feelings and sensations that were impossible to communicate through words. Unfortunately, filming went all wrong from the very beginning, and as Brooks Clift recalled, this picture "killed" his brother, destroying what was left of his career and making him a "living corpse."[22]

Huston asked existentialist philosopher Jean-Paul Sartre, whom he had met in Paris six years before while he was filming *Moulin Rouge,* to write a screenplay. "I considered him the ideal man…. He had read psychology deeply, knew Freud's work intimately and would have an objective and logical approach."[23] Sartre accepted Huston's proposal either because of the deep interest and knowledge he had of Freud or for the money. The philosopher used Ernest Jones' biography on Freud as his main source, as well as the personal correspondence and works of the psychiatrist. Sartre wrote a 2000 page script, which meant that it would be a 10-hour-long film. It was ridiculous and, of course, unacceptable. The director and writer then met at Huston's home in Ireland to try and review it, but after long and exhausting conversations often interrupted by many arguments, Sartre decided to rewrite it. But Huston again was not satisfied with the final result and asked old friends and screenwriters Wolfgang Reinhardt and Charles Kaufman to do the work. Then, Sartre required that he not be mentioned in the film credits even though the film was based on his original script.

Once Monty had signed his contract, he started to work on his character by reading Jones' biography on Freud and by asking questions of Freudian psychologist Dr. Silverberg. At the beginning of August, Monty traveled to London with Claude for a costume fitting with designer Doris Langley Moor and then visited John Huston in his castle in St. Clarens, Ireland. As a present he brought the director a copy of Freud's *Civilization and Its Discontents* with a dedication: "To John with my best. Tinged with no small amount of admiration and affection. Monty."

Sir Stafford Clark was another guest at Huston's castle. He was one of the most illustrious English psychiatrists, who specialized in Freud and was engaged as the film's medical advisor. Monty annoyed Clark with remarks and questions that were often incomprehensible and said at the wrong moments. It upset Huston. "I should have dropped Monty right then but I didn't. I thought that when we got on the set and he had the lines he would be all right. I was mistaken."[24]

The script was constantly revised and Monty objected to the last minute revisions, starting new conflicts with Huston. The fracture between the two became unbridgeable when Huston unexpectedly came into Monty and Claude's room and discovered them having sex. Huston apparently was revolted, as he was incredibly unaware of Monty's homosexuality. A different version of the incident has Monty in bed with a director's assistant or a journalist, and it would better explain Huston's rage.

Freud started to be filmed in Munich on September 11, 1961. Monty arrived there after an animated flight. On board he was drunk and caused a scene with Lufthansa's flight attendants because he refused to fasten his seat belt and they had to hold him down physically for the entire trip. The news was in all of the German newspapers, disgusting Huston.

Every day the situation became more tense, and every little excuse would result in an argument between actor and director. Monty later stated, "I had to play Freud both as a patient, which he was, and a doctor. The lines needed immediacy to keep the audience caring. Every time there was a break to explain something the audience would be lost. Many of the lines given me, I simply couldn't say: they made no sense."[25] And Huston wrote in his autobiography: "Finally I realized this was primarily a stall for time. Monty was having difficulty memorizing his lines. I was surprised at this because he had done so well during *The Misfits*."[26] Quarrels over the interpretation of the film were endless, making shooting extremely difficult. It was a daily struggle that Huston would usually win due to Monty's exhaustion.

Susannah York played Cecily Koertner, a sexually repressed patient of Freud's. She sided with Monty, as did all the women in the cast. She was convinced that his body's decadence was worsened by Huston's continuous humiliations. "I liked Monty enormously right away ... he was extremely generous, and extremely forthcoming [but also] a very incredibly difficult

Monty playing the father of psychoanalysis with Eric Portman in a scene from John Huston's ***Freud,*** 1962.

person, a very very difficult neurotic man to deal with."[27] York was cast after Marilyn Monroe turned down the part, as she had been advised to do by her analyst Dr. Ralph Greenson, who didn't believe a film about Freud should be made because Freud's daughter Anna opposed the project. Later after seeing the picture Greenson admitted that he was wrong considering that the picture was very serious and made more from a scientific point of view.[28]

Huston would use any kind of trick to annoy Monty. He would give him lines the evening before a scene was to be shot, expecting him to memorize them that night. "The script was constantly being rewritten. I would be handed two and half pages at two thirty to be expected to go on camera at four thirty. I was in every scene except one, so I could never take off a few days like the rest of the cast. Sometimes I would be handed a new script at the end of a day's shooting and be expected to have it for the next morning."[29]

Huston insisted that it was Monty's lack of memory. "I had to write his lines on boards and — even having rehearsed the scene — put the lines down on the labels of bottles, door frames and other objects around the set so that he could move around and arrive at a spot where, on cue, the line would be there for him to read."[30]

The European press spread rumors about the chaotic atmosphere on the set. Monty was always described as the troublemaker, often drunk with no memory, who had made the movie run over budget because of his lateness on the set.

In one of the last scenes in the picture, Freud is having a lecture about the Oedipus complex in front of a hostile audience. One of the extras was supposed to hit Freud's top hat and exclaim "Dirty Jew!" The stroke accidentally scratched Monty in the eye and it made him very worried about possible consequences for his sight. He spent a week in London consulting a specialist who discovered advanced cataracts in both eyes, but for medical reasons they could not to be operated on until a year after the diagnosis. Monty wanted to sue Universal, but his brother Brooks made him change his mind. "Now I suppose we'll have to get him a seeing-eye dog for Christmas to lead him!" Huston joked cynically, when he received a telegram from Monty updating him on the health of his eyes.

After a month of filming in Munich's Geisellesteig Studios, the set moved to Vienna to shoot some outdoor scenes. There the situation did not change and the Austrian crew was more impatient with Monty's problems. Some even thought of organizing an authentic boycott, because he was once again playing a Jew; after making *The Young Lions* and *Judgment at Nuremberg,* people were wondering if he wasn't actually Jewish.

The peak of the tension was reached when Huston tried a last desperate attempt to make him memorize his lines. He went to Monty's dressing room, opened the door and slammed it so hard that a mirror fell from the wall and shattered. With a blank expression on his face, Monty looked at Huston for a moment and then said, "What are you trying to do … kill me?" "I'm seriously considering it," answered the director angrily.[31]

During rehearsal of the dream scene in which Monty had to climb up a slope toward his mother in a long dark corridor using a rope, there was no dialogue. The rope burned the palms of his hands, but Huston made Monty do it repeatedly, even though he could see him in pain. A few days later the director and star were together at a social dinner, and Huston noticed Monty's hands. "Did I do that to you?" he asked candidly. And Monty using his deepest voice replied, "Son of a bitch!"

On December 13, 1961, a gala premiere of *Judgment at Nuremberg* was held in West Berlin. Monty again met with Judy Garland, Maximilian Schell, Marlene Dietrich and Spencer Tracy. Stanley Kramer organized a large, shrewd publicity campaign inviting at his expense over 300 reporters from all over the world, including more than 100 from New York alone. Furthermore, Berlin's mayor and future German chancellor Willy Brandt gave a brief speech, but the audience's reaction to the film was not very enthusiastic.

Monty attended the event with his long, Freudian beard and he was completely drunk and stoned, giving a pitiful image of himself. He crawled around on his hands and knees between the aisles of the theatre, screaming out all sorts of crazy things and laughing hysterically. As soon as he saw Spencer Tracy entering the theater, Monty jumped on his back screaming "Yippee," embarrassing everyone in the room and forcing Tracy to leave right after the screening due to the pain he had carelessly inflicted upon his back.

Once back to work in Munich, Monty heard the bad news that Huston had given up hope of saving the film from extra delays and on containing the expenses which had already reached over $600,000.

Monty's troubles with *Freud* did not end when the film was completed in February 1962. Previously, Universal had some doctors and psychiatrists visit Monty to determine his real physical and mental condition in the hopes of then suing him for being irresponsible in his behavior and for the picture going over budget. The Fireman's Fund Insurance, which was the same company that paid for the delays on *Raintree County,* had Monty examined again and the diagnosis was that he was suffering from anxiety caused by worrying too much about his cataracts.

The making of *Freud* took over five months and it cost $4 million, which was exactly double the time and the budget originally allotted. Then Universal decided to cut off Monty's salary, and the actor sued them for $131,000 that was left unpaid. The studio then countersued for $686,000, claiming Monty's misconduct was the main reason that the movie went overbudget. Universal lost the case and Monty obtained the remainder of his salary, but the negative publicity around him increased his reputation as a troublemaker and an uninsurable actor.

Freud was a hit only in New York, because, many thought, it was too much of an artistic film and did not perform well with general audiences. Despite what had happened during the filming Huston stated after the movie was completed: "It was impossible not to marvel at and admire his talent. Monty's eyes would light up, and you could actually 'see' an idea being born in 'Freud's' mind. Monty looked intelligent. He looked as though he were having a thought. He wasn't, Christ knows."[32] Then years later he added: "I saw *Freud* again recently ... [Monty's] genius shows through, and in the end I think he gives quite an extraordinary performance."[33]

A few days after his return from Europe, Monty was hospitalized at Mount Sinai Hospital in New York to undergo a hernia operation and to have some varicose veins removed in his legs. His health was not getting any better and his jaw was causing him pain, forcing him to see a dentist for treatment every week. He would rarely go out with the exception of paying a visit to Nancy Walker, Nan Huston or Marilyn Monroe.

Marilyn would often invite him for dinner on Tuesdays or Thursdays when her Italian maid, Lena Pepitone, was cooking Italian dishes for her. "Montgomery Clift would come for dinner and not eat anything. He was very skinny and he'd drink only vodka. When I used to serve his plate at the table, he'd just stare at it for the entire dinner or he'd hide his face with his hands. Marilyn would beg him to eat but he'd just shake his head without saying a word. The long conversations they used to have in their meetings were always about psychiatrists and sleeping pills they were both taking."[34]

On August 6, 1962, Marilyn died of an apparent overdose of sleeping pills; Monty was devastated. "She was one of the greatest actresses ever. She gave so much. How she gave. Working with her was like an escalator, the give-and-take was fantastic. You'd meet her at one level, then she'd rise to here and you'd meet her, and then higher. I've never encountered such a give-and-take in twenty-eight years."[35]

Monty was frightened all of his colleagues recently dying and confessed to a friend, "Death always comes in threes in show business, first Gable now Marilyn. Who will be next?"[36]

In December Claude accompanied him to have the first of his two cataract operations. After it, Monty told his brother, Brooks, that he felt better and that he trusted the surgeon, even though he was still scared of becoming permanently blind. Ten days after this, a second operation was performed successfully. His mother visited him at the hospital and although Monty did not want to see her, he finally hugged her, cried and said, "Oh Ma, give me your strength, I need your strength."[37]

At home he started reading a few scripts that he was still receiving. He turned down *Antonia,* a film to be directed by Vittorio De Sica and produced by Carlo Ponti, opposite Sophia Loren. He explained his dissatisfaction with screen treatments. "Those who know me in the industry are aware that my first consideration is and always will be the story. I have not always guessed right in this respect, but I have never made a film [of] which I was ashamed."

He would have played a deaf mute in *The Heart Is a Lonely Hunter,* based on Carson McCullers' novel, but when his new agent Robert Lantz contacted 20th Century–Fox, they told him that they were not interested in a uninsurable actor with a bad reputation.

So Monty was forced to be unemployed and his alcohol and drug problem continued, this time associated with a compulsion for anonymous sex. Frank Taylor was one of the few friends who stayed by his side. Every day after work he'd stop at Monty's to see how he was doing. The last time they saw each other was on the occasion of one of Monty's sexual adventures. After a dinner with Monty and Claude, Taylor drove in a limo with them to a sinister gay bar called Dirty Dick's on Christopher Street in Greenwich Village. After they went inside and while he was waiting in the car, a police vehicle approached him and asked if he knew Montgomery Clift, because if so, it was strongly advised that he go and get him out before trouble started. Taylor was worried and ran into the place only to find Monty in the back room stretched out on a table fully clothed, but surrounded by a group of 30 people, including drag-queens, lesbians and gays in leather, who were touching him and kissing him everywhere, as if it were an orgiastic rite. "It was the most debauched scene I've ever witnessed."[38]

In October another episode saddened Monty's life. His twenty-one-year-old niece Suzanne, Brooks' daughter, was arrested for shooting her boyfriend Piero Brentani, whose baby she was carrying. The press did not forget to mention Monty in the scandal that had hit the Clift family, and his townhouse was besieged by reporters looking for his statement. The tragedy united the family and Bill Clift (who took over all the trial expenses for his granddaughter) reconciled with his son. His parents visited him, for the first time after he had moved into his new house with Claude.

It was traumatic for Bill Clift to face his son's homosexuality, but he eventually accepted it. They were willing to help Monty with his drug problems and chronic alcoholism, but they realized that the presence of Claude was detrimental to their son's health. Sunny contacted Billy LeMassena to get advice on how to help her son with his addictions and how to keep him from destroying himself. She hoped that through LeMassena's personal experience with AA, Monty could resolve his problems. Billy tried to convince Monty to come with him to the AA meetings, but it was a useless effort. Monty kept saying that he could quit any time, a fantasy that he shared with Dr. Silverberg, who was still maintaining that his patient was not an alcoholic.

One evening Billy went to see Monty; he was already sleeping, so he briefly talked with Claude. At one point, the Frenchman left the room; after some time he returned looking pale saying that he was tired of living and fed up with his relationship with Monty and for this reason he had just taken a bottle of sleeping pills. LeMassena, in panic, was about to call an ambulance, when Claude laughed and said that he was joking.

The next morning Monty received an early call from Billy, who asked how Claude was doing. Monty replied that he did not know because he had not seen him yet. Billy told him what had happened the night before and Monty let the phone drop and went dashing off to him. A couple of minutes later he was back on the phone screaming that Claude was dead.

Perrin was not dead but in a deep coma as Dr. Ludwig diagnosed before transferring him to Grace Square Hospital where he stayed for several weeks. Before he was discharged, the doctors insisted that Monty and he split up, for both their sakes.[39]

NINE

Oblivion

"Who, sir, shall I autograph this to?"
"Write it to me, dear, my name is Monty Clift!"
— *Kim Novak*

After Claude's suicide attempt, Monty became very depressed and his health worsened dramatically. He was living in a state of perennial tension that forced him to stay at home and to avoid any social occasions. He would seldom go out, and if he did, it was only to take a walk in his neighborhood. It was a pitiful sight for all of his neighbors who knew him as a Hollywood star, not as the completely unrecognizable person he was now.

"His body was rigid, his movements constricted. And the face was a mask; the eyes were dull. He could hardly walk. A friend led him by the elbow. His hands trembled. He stumbled slightly as he moved along. He seemed as if he were in trance, as if he were no longer with us, as if his overwhelming personal isolation was irremediable. And I remember thinking: he is a dead man."[1]

With those words, journalist Ralph Zucker remembered Monty who was living on the Upper East Side at the time. One day while Monty was walking in front of his home, he recognized his neighbor, actress Kim Novak, and asked for her autograph. While she held the pencil to paper she asked, "Who, sir, shall I autograph this to?" Monty shrugged and said, "Write it to me, dear, my name is Monty Clift!" When she got over the shock, Kim Novak embraced him, took out her lavender ink pen and wrote: "With love, Kim."

Dr. Ludwig apprehensively expressed all of his concerns about Monty's health to Monty's lawyer Jack Clareman and to the agent Robert Lantz, whose help the physician wanted in order to convince Monty to be hospitalized. Monty demanded that the matter be discussed in the presence of Dr. Silverberg, who declared himself against it. Then the psychiatrist told Bill Clift, "My dear sir, if that man gets out of my control he'll die within three months."[2] For the sake of her son, Sunny Clift considered moving into his house to personally take care of him, but she was persuaded not to by Dr. Ludwig, because he was sure that the cohabitation would become a nightmare. A better solution was taken; a professional nurse was hired. Lorenzo "Larry" James, a black former singer and actor, was recommended by Dr. Ludwig after consultation with Billy LeMassena and Sunny.

Larry proved himself very loyal from the beginning; he moved into the house to take care of Monty 24 hours a day. He would put Monty to bed, massage him, make him feel comfortable and often take him to see a movie or for a walk. His legs were very weak and painful because he was suffering from a grave form of phlebitis that made him walk and move in an uncoordinated manner. The most intensive treatment that Monty had in those days was for hypoparathyroidism, a rare hormonal pathology that afflicted people like Monty who already suffered from problems of the thyroid.

With Larry's help, Monty was able to see some of his old friends like Nancy Walker, Roddy McDowall, Donald Windham and Sandy Campbell. They all noticed how much Monty was suffering from being unpopular and unrecognizable on the street.

One night Robert Thom invited him to dinner at a new Polynesian restaurant located in the Savoy Plaza. At the end of the meal Monty insisted on paying the check, and because he was one of the sponsors of the restaurant, when the check arrived he just signed it as was his custom. His signature had become illegible due to his illnesses. The waiter came back and asked if he had any identification, because he obviously did not recognize him. Monty was shaken. He took off his glasses and gazed up at the waiter and said: "Only my face." The waiter was at a loss. He conferred with the headwaiter who was equally bewildered. He did not want to offend a customer, but he did not know who Monty was. So Thom told Monty, "You are a son of a bitch; don't embarrass the poor bastard. Tell him who you are or let me pay the check with cash." But Monty was still immovable. Finally a manager supplied the right words, his name, and apologies were made and they left.[3]

Truman Capote witnessed another significant episode.

> He phoned me and invited me to lunch. "I can't," I said, "because I haven't done any Christmas shopping." He said, "Listen I haven't bought anything

either. If you take me shopping with you, I'll buy you lunch." So I met him at his house and we walked to the Colony. He seemed perfectly normal and full of good humor, and we were laughing and having a fine time. No one could have been more charming.... When we finished eating, we went shopping at an Italian store that specialized in beautiful, expensive sweaters. At lunch he had had just one drink — one drink! But he must have shot up or taken pills in the men's room, because suddenly he went utterly, completely to pieces, just like an insane person. He pointed to the counter, where all the sweaters were stacked, and counted, "One, two, three, four, five ... sixteen. How much are all of those?" The salesman told him and Monty picked up all of the sweaters in one huge bundle — there were so many they were falling out of his arms — and somehow got the door open. It had begun to rain by this time — in fact it was pouring — but he walked out and threw them all in the gutter. When he came back, the salesman just asked, "And to what address do I send the bill, Mr. Clift?" I've never seen anyone so cool in my life as the salesman. Monty wouldn't speak to him.... "Monty you've got to go home," I said when we went outside. "I'm not going anywhere!" he replied, and we began to have a struggle in the street. I shoved him into the back seat of a taxi, but he got out, walked around the back and got into the front seat, where he tried to grab the wheel away from the driver, who told us to get out or [he would] call the police. "Oh please God, do anything except that!" I said. "This man is very ill. Take him to this address, and I'll give you a big tip. Please! ..." I was holding Monty, who was screaming and shouting. It was a nightmare. When we got to his house, his colored houseman managed to get him inside and called his doctor, who gave him an injection.[4]

Larry's constant presence proved to be good. Now Monty also enjoyed staying at home and doing things he had given up for a long time. He studied graphology and showed an interest in learning about astrology with the guidance of a famous British astrologer. Once again he started to read the newspapers every day, especially the British ones, and started listening to his favorite music by Frank Sinatra and Ella Fitzgerald. He was so fond of their songs that every time someone suggested that he listen to other singers he would ask innocently, "Who?" He had such respect for Billie Holiday that he would say, "Oh I can't listen to her" because Holiday's suffering was so vast, so moving, that he could not bear it.[5]

Five months later Monty's health and spirit improved enormously. Larry had been doing a great job, earning not only Monty's total trust as a patient but also becoming a real friend to him. Monty would leave him thank you notes on the house staircase as he used to do with Marge Stengel when she was in London with him during the filming of *Suddenly Last Summer*. They were little and infantile signs of the great sensitivity and fragility of a man who had been abandoned to a cruel destiny too early.

Monty at forty-five years old, looking pre-maturely aged, 1965.

Larry met all the members of Monty's family and found them all to be very unhappy with themselves. At the time, Bill Clift was in the hospital because of a heart attack. He died some days later in February 1964. Sunny kept her children out of Bill's hospital room, and they impassively accepted their mother's orders, confirming to Larry how big and intrusive Sunny's presence still was in her children's lives. The only one who seemed more "normal" was Ethel, probably because she had been living in Texas for years and she no longer submitted to her mother's authority.

After Bill Clift died, Monty gave his mother a monthly allow-ance. It was not easy for Sunny to be financially dependent on her son, considering that she had always been "the column" of the Clift family.

In the spring of 1966 Monty met Elizabeth Taylor, who was in New York because her husband Richard Burton was acting on Broadway in John Gielgud's production of *Hamlet*. Monty accompanied her to the premiere of John Huston's *The Night of the Iguana* and later to a benefit at the Lunt-Fontanne Theatre, where Burton and Taylor read some poetry to collect funds for the New York Drama and Music Academy. That night, Monty met a lot of people from show business, including old friends like Lee Remick and Myrna Loy. He surprised everybody by being in great shape and spirits.

Elizabeth was convinced that he was finally ready to return to work. Burton's success on Broadway had awakened his interest in the Shake-speare plays, which he brought with him when he left the following sum-mer for a vacation to Fire Island at the gay resort, The Pines. There Monty would rarely go out of the garden of his rented villa. He was seriously try-ing to determine if he could produce one of Shakespeare's plays.

"To wit that Monty was drunk the entire time he was in the Pines.

Totally false! The injuries Monty sustained in that automobile accident in Hollywood had resulted in constant pain, impairment of vision and balance controlled by the inner ear. Consequently, he developed a particular way of walking that led people to wrong conclusions," recalls Dorothy Levy, who would often meet Monty during his walks on the island.[6]

At the end of the summer while back in town, Monty often went out with record producer Ben Bagley, whom he had met through Robert Thom a couple of months earlier. One night Bagley invited him to a show based on Cole Porter's songs. At the end of the performance they had dinner together and went back to Monty's home. The actor asked him to spend the night with him. "I accepted right away. He told me, 'Wait, let me first show you the real Montgomery Clift,' and he went up to his bedroom. He came back wearing instead of contact lenses a pair of thick glasses. I did not care. I had a crush on him since I first saw him at a show in 1954 with Mira Rostova and Kevin McCarthy. We just cuddled in bed; there was not real sexual intercourse because his physical conditions did not allow it."[7]

It was the beginning of a new friendship that lasted until Monty's death and became very useful. When Larry got hepatitis, Ben often substituted for him. Bagley had the idea of producing a compilation of songs sung by famous actors and had chosen Jerome Kern's *I Have a Room Above* for Monty. The project did not work because Columbia's recording studios were only available in the morning and it was impossible for Monty to work before noon. Then Monty suggested that Bagley replace him with Anthony Perkins, who recently had done a record of French songs. And so it was Perkins who eventually performed Monty's song.

His friendship with Bagley had a stormy moment after Monty spent his second summer at Fire Island in 1965. There he would host some male, Hispanic prostitutes, since they were his favorite type of men. They were often hustlers who would take advantage of his generosity and they would steal from the house or they would try to blackmail him. One of them challenged Monty to run naked along Third Avenue. He did run naked but, thanks to the intervention of his attorney, the story was not printed in the newspapers. Another young man was often seen outside his townhouse at night screaming that he was Monty's illegitimate son, born from a relationship with a married woman.[8]

At that time, the list of bizarre people hanging around his life included a special character, Baroness Irmgard Gassler. She met him in Vienna on the set of *Freud*. Gassler had such a crush on him that she decided to leave Austria to follow him to the United States. The baroness first went to Hollywood, where after a long investigation and Burt Lancaster's help, she was able to obtain Monty's address in New York. One day she came to his door and declared her love for him. Monty invited her inside, where she showed him a big scrapbook with tons of articles about and photographs of him.

From then on she would write to him long love letters daily and visit him periodically from Austria. Gassler would take him out for dinner or to the theater and she even proposed marriage to the totally uninterested Monty. Sunny received a bouquet of flowers from her with a note signed "from your future daughter-in-law." When Gassler's brother arrived in New York, she "offered" him to Monty "as a present" because "he is young and handsome and will be very very kind."[9]

Her house in Innsbruck had all the walls covered with Monty's photographs and she would play a record called "Monty's Potpourri" non-stop. It was a compilation of her idol's favorite songs that he had had made exclusively for him in 1952; he had given a copy to her.

After Monty's death, Gassler self-published a memoir of their relationship. "He is mine and he belongs to me and in our last telepathic conversation we exchanged once again words filled with our love."[10]

Finally, after a break of two and half years, Monty was ready to go back to work, so he accepted two offers. His first commitment was to participate in a recording of Tennessee Williams' drama *The Glass Menagerie* directed by Harvey Sackler for Caedmon's Theater Recording Society. Monty played the part of Tom Wingfield opposite Julie Harris and Jessica Tandy. Although his voice was not like it used to be, his talent allowed him to attain excellent results by using a technique based on a perfect balance of pauses and silence.

Then he narrated *William Faulkner's Mississippi*, a WNEW-TV documentary (produced by Robert Guenette who directed in 1989 an interesting documentary on Monty) that looks at Faulkner's southern heritage and examines his writing for an interpretation of the reasons for Southern resistance to desegregation. Faulkner was also one of Monty's favorite authors, and he specially admired *As I Lay Dying*. In this instance his husky voice was able to express very emotional feelings through the use of high and low tones which proved very effective, especially in describing racial acts committed against black people. His interpretation was, in fact, unanimously praised by critics.

On August 20, 1965, Monty made a will: 60 percent of his estate was left to his sister, Ethel, and the remaining 40 percent to his mother, Sunny. He also included certain legacies such as one for $12,500 to Brooks, two for $5,000 to Mira Rostova and Marge Stengel, one for $3,000 to Lorenzo James and others for $500 to friends like Anne Lincoln and his former cook Elizabeth Guenster.

A couple of months later Brooks announced his fourth marriage with Eleanor Roeloffs. Monty gladly accepted the invitation to be his best man and offered his house for the wedding reception. He organized the ceremony with Larry's help, personally ordering the flowers and champagne, while Sunny took care of the catering.

Later in December Eleanor had a baby, and Brooks asked his brother if he could name him Edward Montgomery. Monty was deeply moved, knowing he would never have children, and gave his nephew a check that Brooks never cashed. Instead he framed it as a memento.

Elizabeth Taylor was always someone whom Monty could count on. They did not see each other as often as they used to and Monty complained about this in an interview with *Cosmopolitan.* "I have not seen her since she was to marry Victor Mature."[11] He always knew she was there for him, and the proof of this was that she was trying hard to help him get back to work in a film with her.

After filming *Cleopatra,* Taylor had great power in Hollywood. Warner Brothers wanted her in *Reflections in a Golden Eye* based on Carson McCullers' novel. It was the story of a married, homosexually repressed Army colonel who was obsessed with a young officer, who in turn was infatuated with the unsatisfied wife of his superior. Elizabeth liked the script and accepted the part on the condition that Monty was cast in it as well. Producer Roy Stark reminded her that Monty was uninsurable and that it would be impossible to cast him. But Elizabeth did not give up and offered her own salary, about $1 million, as insurance if Monty was unreliable. Taylor also wanted Richard Burton to direct the film, but she could not convince the producer, so John Huston was hired as director. "Everything will be fine, you'll see," Monty said to Huston's assistant Doc Erickson in order to reassure him that a traumatic experience like *Freud* could not happen again.[12] But the filming of *Reflections in a Golden Eye* was postponed to a date to be determined once Elizabeth was free from her previous obligations.

Monty found himself spending long days without a job in which he was willing to give everything. He was finally ready to again feel those sensations that only acting could give him. Lee Strasberg offered him a part in Chekhov's *Three Sisters,* which would open in London shortly. But acting on stage was still frightening to him, so he refused it.

He repainted the façade of his townhouse with Ben Bagley's help, installing some bright orange awnings on the outside of the building that his neighbors complained were too flashy.

Suddenly, out of the blue, Monty received a call from his old friend Salka Viertel, who had first contacted Jack Larson to see if Monty would possibly be interested in *The Great Illusion,* a script by Raoul Levy, for which he had Monty in mind to play the protagonist. Levy had become popular after he made *Et Dieu Créa la Femme,* a film that launched Brigitte Bardot as an international star. Monty understood that the picture could be the vehicle for his return to the big screen and that it could also prove to the producers that he was still able to act in a major role (his idea was to obtain the part in *Reflections in a Golden Eye* that was being produced by Warner Bros. too). Long and exhausting phone calls between Europe and New York were made, focusing mostly on Monty's insurability after he passed several medical tests taken by Warners, who were still not convinced about his health, in particular his sanity.

He tried to stay fit as much as he could and also had cosmetic surgery to remove the bags and lines under his eyes. This surgery was badly performed by surgeon Dr. Manfred Von Linde, who left him with a scar on his cheek and an infection on his eyelids.

Over the holiday, he flew down to Austin, Texas, to visit his sister and went with her family to ski in Red River, New Mexico, stopping for a couple of days in Santa Fe.

After New Year's he went to London to visit Leslie Caron, Warren Beatty's girlfriend at the time. She had been chosen by Raoul Levy to star opposite Monty in their upcoming movie, which had now been renamed *The Defector.* In the beginning, the director had cast Italian actress Monica Vitti, but after reading the script she turned it down.

The task of finding a star to act opposite Monty found another obstacle at the end of January, when Caron left the set because she did not get along with the director. Caron wrote a letter to Monty:

> My dear Monty,
>
> I have been terribly upset by all this, and I'm sure you
> resent my walking away. You must think I did you a bad
> turn, but you know when I read my last script, my part has
> been so diminished in importance ... but I think, the script,
> as a whole, makes more sense and I think you and Kruger
> will come out of it very well.
> I'm so glad that you managed to clear up the script, you
> must have worked very hard! ... Good wishes for the film!
>
> Leslie Caron.[13]

While in London Monty tried in vain to convince her friend actress Simon Signoret to take the part. At the end a relatively unknown actress,

Macha Meril, was picked. Levy told her that he had had her in his mind from the very beginning, but Warners' producers had not agreed.

The Defector's cast included Monty's faithful friend Roddy McDowall in the part of a CIA agent and in smaller roles, French director Jean-Luc Godard and German actor Hardy Krüger.

Before leaving for Munich where the shooting of the film began, Monty asked Mira Rostova to go with him and Larry and to coach him in his part for his professional rebirth. They stayed in one of the most luxurious suites at the Grand Continent Hotel in Munich. The making of *The Defector* took almost three months due to troubling weather conditions that resulted in rainy and cold days. The script had many action scenes in which the actors had to climb, crawl and bike, as well as dive into a freezing river. Monty insisted on doing all of his stunts without a double. It was his intention to prove to everybody that he was in perfect shape, but it was harmful to his phlebitis and arthritis. At the end of each take he would feel exhausted, and he'd go back to rest, making Levy extremely nervous about the frequent interruptions. "He gives so much it is almost painful ... almost as though he were acting to destroy himself," recalls co-star Macha Meril.[14]

In his last interview before he died, Monty told Anthony Haden-Guest, an editor from the *New York Journal Tribune*: "Four years, four years without making a picture! Now that is terrible when you get to my age because how can you grow unless you work? ... But these four years haven't been entirely fruitless. I did some living. And getting to know myself. And I did some traveling to England to see Larry Olivier's *Othello* and to the Caribbean, although I didn't really feel that I deserved a vacation. But now! ... Now I do!"[15]

Levy was very satisfied with Monty's work. He admired him and thought that his acting had improved compared to the past when his striking beauty prevented impartial judgment of his professional qualities. Unfortunately, the director died shortly afterwards. He was having a nervous breakdown because his girlfriend had broken up with him. One day he knocked at the door of her hotel room where she was staying, carrying a loaded rifle. There was a violent fight and Levy was found dead with a bullet in his chest.

When the picture was completed, Monty left with Larry for London, where Leslie Caron threw a party in his honor, inviting celebrities like Warren Beatty, Sharon Tate and Barbra Streisand, who was very eager to meet him. In London, Monty met some of his old friends like Betsy Blair, and Susannah York who accompanied him to see a Shakespearean play at Stratford on Avon. He also visited Fred Zinnemann, who was filming *A*

Man for All Seasons. The director was shocked by Monty's appearance. "He looked like a dying man," Zinnemann later recalled. All the actors in the cast wanted to talk to him, honored to meet one of Hollywood's legendary stars.[16]

When Monty returned home he received the news that the filming of *Reflections in a Golden Eye* would start in Rome on September 15. The script had been adapted by a young screenwriter named Francis Ford Coppola, who was just beginning his career.

Monty's body began to feel the aftereffects of making *The Defector*. Closer friends like Billy LeMassena and Ben Bagley witnessed his painful physical decay, which Monty was trying to stop with Demerol injections. He was very moody and prone to sudden attacks of hysteria, even around people who loved him, like Larry, whom he no longer trusted. According to Marge Stengel, Lorenzo James was not only assisting Monty as a nurse and personal secretary but had established a sort of sexual relationship with his employer similar to the one shown in Joseph Losey's film *The Servant*, one of Monty's favorite pictures. He was anxious to make *Reflections in a Golden Eye* and felt that working was the best medication to save him from sadness and gloom.

On July 12, 1966, Monty spent the entire day at home. At 1:00 a.m. Larry entered his room to ask him if he wanted to watch *The Misfits* which was on TV. "Absolutely not" was his answer. The next day at sunrise Larry went to wake him up; Monty usually fell into a very deep sleep and needed to be shaken in order to be woken up. He found him dead, lying naked in bed, still wearing glasses. "Mr. Clift had a habit of falling asleep with his glasses on," Larry explained to the police later.

His attempts to wake him up were unsuccessful, so in a state of shock he called Dr. Ludwig, but he was unable to reach him because the physician was out of town. His associate Dr. Howard Kline rushed over to the house and pronounced Monty dead from a heart attack. His body was taken to the city morgue where Dr. Michael Baden conducted the autopsy. He did not find any evidence of alcohol in his blood and concluded that Mr. Clift had died of occlusive coronary artery disease.

Many rumors about his death started to circulate. One was that Dr. Von Linde had given him lethal medication, after sneaking into the house while Larry was away. Another one included disgusting comments on the size of Monty's genitalia, which Dr. Baden made during a party.[17] These details were previously also reported by author Kenneth Anger in his scandalous book *Hollywood Babylonia*, but the actor was able to remove the comment from the final version of the book thanks to his attorneys.

A couple of days before dying, Monty called Nancy Walker and promised to meet her at Fire Island the following weekend. Another rumor surrounding his death was that Monty actually died on Fire Island and was brought back into the city before his death was reported.

Sunny was informed by Larry immediately, along with all of Monty's closest friends. Roddy McDowall burst into tears and called Elizabeth Taylor and Richard Burton in London, where they were filming *The Taming of the Shrew*. For Elizabeth the loss was devastating. "He was like a brother to me, it was my dearest friend."

Taming of Shrew's director Franco Zeffirelli remembers: "Elizabeth wanted to go [to Monty's funeral] but such a rupture in the schedule was unthinkable to a professional like Liz. Even that day after her sobbing had died down, she went on the set."[18]

Richard Burton wrote in his diaries: "His companion, nurse and major domo very kindly sent Elizabeth his [Monty's] handkerchiefs which he had only recently bought in Paris and which he loved, delicate white on white. And to me — Monty's favorite soap. I didn't know him very well but he seemed a good man. Elizabeth has received a couple of lovely letters from his mother."[19]

Ethel organized the service at St. James Episcopal Church on Madison Avenue on July 26th in the form of a private funeral. Sunny, Brooks, Ethel and Larry sat in the front row; around them were Mira Rostova, Nancy Walker, Donald Windham, Sandy Campbell, Billy LeMassena, Ned Smith, Bobby Lewis, Jerome Robbins, Dore Schary and Lauren Bacall. Libby Holman was accompanied by her sons Jim and Tony and made a generous contribution to the Motion Picture Relief Fund in Monty's memory.

Libby also wrote a moving sympathy card to Sunny: "We are grieved that Monty is not with us any more. It was a great pleasure and a deep gratification to have known a human being like him. He will always be like a bright shining sun to my family and me. I send you my sympathy and gratitude having made it possible for us to know him."[20]

Inside the church there were two large bouquets of white chrysanthemums from Elizabeth Taylor with a note, "Rest perturbed spirit," and also a nice floral arrangement sent by Roddy McDowall, who was working in Hollywood.

"What a terrible loss! He had so much potential, but he just couldn't manage it. Everything got to him. He needed a few more layers of skin to cope with this mad world."[21] Those were the words in Myrna Loy's message with the flowers she sent.

Donald Coats, the organist, played a selection of Monty's favorite music pieces at the ceremony, mostly from Bach.

The burial was held at a little gravesite in the Quakers' Friends Cemetery inside Brooklyn's Prospect Park, a beautiful peaceful solitary place. His grave stands close to his father's. The tombstone was engraved with his name and date of birth and it was made by John Benson, Ned Smith's nephew, who also made President John F. Kennedy's gravestone at Arlington.

Monty's estate was valued at $200,000 and distributed according to his will. The townhouse on 61st Street was sold by Ethel to a couple, friends of Robert Lantz, under the condition that they affix a bronze plaque to the façade that said, "Residence of Montgomery Clift, Actor 1920–1966."

Newspapers from all over the world wrote obituaries, but the most interesting and surprising was one by *L'Osservatore della Domenica,* a weekly magazine published by Vatican City. "Montgomery Clift died and lived alone and nobody will ever know the secret of his secretive, sad and tortured life. We shall not recall or judge on aspects of his life that were or seemed questionable. But it is a fact that there was in his lonely existence an example to remember, the example of his integrity as an artist, of his disinterestedness of his contempt for easy success!"

Another poignant remembrance was written by Vittorio De Sica in the *Times* of London.

> I had the honor and pleasure to work with Montgomery Clift in a film entitled *Indiscretion of an American Wife,* and so to know him well — intimately. He was the most sensitive, intelligent actor I have ever known. He played his roles with a sense of poetry. I remember that he loved children — and was himself one, who thrived on tenderness. But destiny became his enemy; he who was worthy of goodness, of friendship and above all, of happiness. From the time of that horrible auto accident, he never seemed to know peace. As the years passed, it became worse and worse for him. Finally his heart could not contain his enormous desperation, and so it stopped beating. Now we are sadly without that fine actor who gave the world those wonderful and gratifying performances that will remain forever in our memory.
>
> Goodbye, Monty, my friend, my brother.[22]

Four months later *The Defector* was released in theaters and it was poorly received, grossing a modest amount at the box office and receiving terrible reviews. It was the worst way to say goodbye to Monty on the big screen.

In September Marlon Brando took over Monty's role in *Reflections in a Golden Eye.* It was the first Hollywood film to deal with the taboo of homosexuality in an explicit manner.

Appendix 1: Plays

As Husbands Go

A comedy in prologue and three acts, by Rachel Crothers. Non-professional production in Sarasota, Florida, March **1933.**

Montgomery Clift (Wilburn).

Fly Away Home

A comedy in three acts by Dorothy Bennett and Irving White. *Director:* Thomas Mitchell. *Producer:* Theron Bamberg. Stockbridge Massachusetts, Summer stock 1934 and with the same company January 15, **1935,** at 48th St. Theatre, New York. 202 performances.

Cast: Montgomery Clift (Harmer Masters), Georgette McKee (Buff Masters), Joan Tompkins (Linda Masters), Edwin Philips (Corey Masters), Claire Woodbury (Penny), Lili Zehner (Tinka Collingsby), Philip Faversham (Johnny Heming), Thomas Mitchell (James Masters), Albert Van Dekker (Arme Sloan), Geraldine Kay (Maria), Sheldon Leonard (Gabriel), Elmer Brown (Taxi Driver), Ann Mason (Nan Masters).

Jubilee

Musical comedy by Moss Hart. *Music and lyrics:* Cole Porter. *Director:* Hassard Short and Monty Woolley. *Producer:* Sam H. Harris and Max Gordon. Imperial Theatre, New York, October 11, **1935.** 169 performances.

Cast: Melville Cooper (The King), Mary Bole (The Queen), Charles Waters (Prince James), Margaret Adams (Princess Diana), Montgomery Clift (Prince Peter), Jackie Kelk (Prince Rudolph), Richie Ling (Lord Wyndham), Derek Williams (Eric Dare), June Knight (Karen O'Kane), May Boley (Eva Steing), Mark Plant (Charles Rausmiller or Mowgli), Olive Reeves-Smith (Laura Fitzgerald), Charles Broakaw (A Sandwich Man), Ralph Sumpter (Professor

Rexford), Dorothy Fox (The Beach Widow), Leo Chazel (Cabinet Minister), Charles Brokaw (Cabinet Minister), Don Douglas (Life Guard), Albert Amato (Announcer), Harold Murray (Master of Ceremonies), Jack Edwards (The Drunk), Ted Fetter (The Usher), Leo Chazel (Keeper of the Zoo).

The Road to Paradise

Comedy by Frederik Jackson. *Producer:* Jack Linder July 6th–12th, **1936**, Theatre Alden, Jamaica Long Island and July 13th, Theatre Brighton Beaches.

Yr. Obedient Husband

A sentimental comedy in three acts by Horace Jackson. *Director:* John Cromwell. *Producer:* Marwell Productions. Broadhurst Theatre, New York, January 10, **1938.** 8 performances.

> **Cast:** Dame May Witty (Mrs. Scurlock), Brenda Forbes (Mistress Binns), Florence Eldridge (Prue), Frieda Altman (Podd), Fredric March (Richard Steele), Marie Jolie (Elizabeth), Montgomery Clift (Lord Finch), Harold Thomas (Patrick), Walter Jones (Silas Pennyfield), Helena Glenn (Lady Envil), Leslie Austen (Lord Envil), John Pickard (John Gay), Ethel Morrison (Mrs. Howe), A.J. Herbert (Thomas Howe M.P.), Katherine Stewart (Lady Warwick or Mrs. Addison).

Eye on the Sparrow

A comedy in three acts by Maxwell Selser. *Director:* Antoinette Perry (under the pseudonym of John M. Worth). *Producer:* Girvan G. Higgingson. Vanderbilt Theatre May 3, **1938.** 6 performances.

> **Cast:** Montgomery Clift (Philip Thomas), Katherine Deane (Nancy Thomas), Edgard Stehli (Freeman), Barry Sullivan (Roger Sanford), Philip Ober (Ted Strong), Catherine Doucet (Barbara Thomas), Leslie King (Fejac Strode), Pearce Benton (Jim Wright), Stiano Braggiotti (Rostican), Dorothy Francis (Florence Audgen), Francesca Lenni (O'Mara), Edward Fielding (Thomas Hosea), Ernest Woodward (Rent Collector), Lester Damon (Moving Man), Sey Strouse (Rug Man).

The Wind and the Rain

A comedy in three acts by Merton Hodge. *Director:* Charles J. Parsons. Millbrook Theatre, Millbrook, NY, July 25–30, **1938.** 6 performances.

> **Cast:** Shirley DeMe (Mrs. McPhe), Lex Lindsay (Gilbert Raymond), James Gregory (John Williams), Montgomery Clift (Charles Tritton), Allan Tower (Dr. Paul Duhamel), Evelyn Evers (Anne Hargreaves), Celeste Holm (Jill Manning), Jeffrey William Clark (Roger Cole), Robin Clapp (Pete Morgan).

Dame Nature

A comedy in three acts by Andre Birabeau. Translated from French by Patricia Collinge. *Director:* Worthington Miner. *Producer:* The Theatre Guild. Booth Theatre, New York, September 26, **1938**. 48 performances.

> **Cast:** Thomas Coffin Cooke (Max), Charles Bellin (Beer, a schoolboy), Frederick Bradlee (Second school boy), Edwin Mills (Third schoolboy), Edwin Cooper (Concierge), Harry Irvine (Doctor Faridet), Lois Hall (Leonie Perrot), Montgomery Clift (Ere Brisac), Morgan James (Batton), Peter Miner (Fourth schoolboy), Kathryn Grill (Nannie), Grace Matthews (Marie), Jessie Royce Leis (Madame Brisac), Onslow Stevens (Monsieur Brisac), Forrest Orr (Forrest Orr), Wilton Graff (Paul Marachal).

The Mother

By Paul Selver and Miles Malleson, from a play by Karel Capek. *Director:* Miles Malleson. *Producer:* Victor Payne Jennings in association with Kathleen Robinson. Lyceum Theatre, New York, April 25, **1939.** 31 performances.

> **Cast:** Alla Nazimova (The Mother), Reginald Bach (The Father), Stephen Ker Appleby (Erew), Carl Norval (George), Alan Brixley (Christopher), Tom Palmer (Peter), Montgomery Clift (Tony), Edward Broadley (The Old Man).

There Shall Be No Night

A drama in three acts by E. Sherwood. *Director:* Alfred Lunt. *Producer:* Playwrights Company and the Theatre Guild. Alvin Theatre, New York, April 29, **1940**. 181 performances.

> **Cast:** Alfred Lunt (Dr. Kaarlo Valkonen), Lynne Fontanne (Mirea Valkonen), Richard Whorf (Dave Corween), Sydney Greenstreet (Uncle Waldemar), Brooks West (Gus Shuman), Montgomery Clift (Erik Valkonen), Elizabeth Fraser (Kaatri Alquist), Maurice Colbourne (Dr. Ziemssen), Edward Raquello (Major Rutkowski), Charles Ansley (Joe Burnett), Thomas Gomez (Ben Gichner), William LeMassena (Frank Olmstead), Claude Horton (Sergeant Gosden), Phyllis Thaxter (Lempi), Charva Chester (Ilma), Ralph Nelson (Camera Man), Robert Downing (Camera Man).

Out of the Frying Pan

A comedy in three acts by Francis Swann. *Director:* Sanford Meisner. *Producer:* Jean Muir and Sanford Meisner. County Theater, Suffern, New York, August 4, **1941**. 7 performances.

> **Cast:** Micheal Strong (George Bodell), Kenneth Tobey (Norman Reese), Mabel Paige (Mrs. Garnet), Montgomery Clift (Tony Dennison), Florence McMichael (Muriel Foster), Peggy Meyer (Kate Ault), Sally Gracie (Marge Benson), Gertrude Beach (Dottie Coburn), Harry Antrim (Mr. Coburn), Percy Kilbride (Mr. Kenny), Tony Manning (Mac), Henry Lawson (Joe).

Mexican Mural

A comedy in "4 panels" by Ramon Naya, directed and produced by Robert Lewis. Chanin Auditorium, New York, April 26, **1942**. About 5 performances.

Cast: (**First Panel**) "Vera Cruz Interior" Wallace House (Rumbero), Priscilla Newton, Robert Leer (Comparas), Perry Wilson (Didi Ruiz), Kathryn Grill (Dona Alex), Montgomery Clift (Lalo Brito), Eda Reiss (Luisa).

(**Second Panel**) "Miracle Painting" Libby Holman (Celestina Ruiz), Terry Dicks (Chelina), Spencer James (Doctor Brito), Gertrude Gilpin (Morena), Henrietta Lovelace (Petra), Mira Rosovskaya or Rostova (Verbena), Norma Chambers (a lady).

(**Third Panel**) "Moonlight Scene" Kevin McCarthy (Mariano Ruiz), Owen Jordon (Miguel Ruiz), Wallace House, Spencer James (Troubadours), David Opatoshu (Mata Hari), Larry Hugo, William LeMassena, Morton Amster (Gold Shirts), Tom Barry, Viola Kates, Priscilla Newton, Robert Leer, and others (People of Vera Cruz).

(**Fourth Panel**) "Patio with Flamingo" Kenneth Tobey (the Redhead), Norma Chambers (Juliana), Viola Kates (Maria Chris).

The Skin of Our Teeth

A comedy in three acts by Thornton Wilder. *Director:* Elia Kazan. *Producer:* Michael Myerberg. Plymouth Theatre, New York, November 18, **1942**. 355 performances.

Cast: Fredric March (Mr. Antrobus), Florence Eldridge (Mrs. Antrobus), Tallulah Bankhead (Lily Sabina), E.G. Marshall (Mr. Fitzpatrick), Remo Buffano (Dinosaur), Erew Rautosheff (Mammoth), Dickie Van Patten (Telegraph Boy), Montgomery Clift (Henry Antrobus), Frances Heflin (Gladys Antrobus), Arthur Griffin (Doctor), Ralph Kellar (Professor), Joseph Smiley (Judge), Ralph Cullinan (Homer), Edith Faversham (Ms. E. Muse), Emily Lorraine (Ms. T. Muse), Eva Mudge Nelson (Ms. Muse), Stanley Prager (Usher), Harry Clark (Usher), Elizabeth Scott (Girl), Patricia Riordan (Girl), Florence Reed (Fortune Teller), Earl Synodor, Carrol Clark, Stanley Weede, Seamas Flynn, Aubrey Fasset, Stephan Cole (Conveners), Morton DaCosta (Broadcast Official), Eula Belle Moore (Hester), Viola Dean (Ivy).

Our Town

A play in three acts by Thornton Wilder. *Director:* Wesley McKee. *Producer:* Ed Harris. City Center Theatre, New York, January 10, **1944**. 24 performances.

Cast: Marc Connelly (Stage Manager), Curtis Cooksey (Dr. Gibbs), Carolyn Hummel (Rebecca Gibbs), Montgomery Clift (George Gibbs), Richard Dalton (Joe Crowell), Roy Robson (Si Crowell), Donald Keyes (Howie Newsome), Ethel Remey (Mrs. Webb), Tebby Rose (Wally Webb), Martha Scott (Emily Webb), Parker Fennelly (Mr. Webb), Arthur Allen (Professor Willard), Alice Hill (woman on the balcony), John Paul (man in the auditorium), Frederica Going (woman in the box), William Swetle (Simon Stimson), Doro Meree (Mrs. Soames), Owen Coll (Constable Warren), Jay Velie (Sam Craig), John Ravold (Joe Stoddard), Walter O'Hill (Mr. Carter).

The Searching Wind

A play in two acts by Lilian Hellman, directed and produced by Herman Shumlin. April 21, **1944.** Fulton Theatre, New York. 326 performances.

    Cast: Dudley Digges (Moses Taney), Montgomery Clift (Samuel Hazen), Alfred Hesse (Ponette), Mercedes Gilbert (Saphronia), Cornelia Otis Skinner (Emily Hazen), Dennis King (Alexeer Hazen), Barbara O'Neil (Catherine Bowman) Edgar Erews (Primo Cameriere), Joseph de Santis (Secondo Cameriere), Walter Kohler (Hotel Manager), William F. Scoeller (Eppler), Eric Latham (Edward Halsey), Eugene Earl (James Sears), Arnold Korff (Count Max von Stammer).

Foxhole in the Parlor

A play in two acts by Elsa Shelley. *Director:* John Haggot. *Producer:* Harry Bloomfield. Booth Theatre, New York, May 23, **1945.** 45 performances.

    Cast: Reginald Beane (Leroy), Russell Hardie (Tom Austen), Ann Lincoln (Vicki King), Flora Campbell (Ann Austen), Raymond Greenleaf (Senator Bowen), Montgomery Clift (Dennis Patterson), Grace Coppin (Kate Mitchell).

You Touched Me!

A romantic comedy in three acts by Tennessee Williams and Donald Windham. *Director and Producer:* Guthrie McClintic in collaboration with Lee Shubert. Booth Theatre, New York, September 25, **1945.** 109 performances.

    Cast: Marianne Stewart (Matilda Rockley), Catherine Willard (Emmie Rockley), Norah Howard (Phoebe), Montgomery Clift (Hadrian), Edmund Gwenn (Cornelius Rockley), Neil Fitzgerald (Reverend Guildford Melton), Freeman Hammond (Policeman).

The Sea Gull

A play in four acts by Anton Chekhov. Adapted from the Russian by Mira Rostova, Kevin McCarthy and Montgomery Clift. *Director:* Norris Houghton. *Producer:* The Phoenix Theater, T. Edward Hambleton, Norris Houghton. Phoenix Theatre, New York, May 11, **1954.** 40 performances.

    Cast: Kevin McCarthy (Boris Trigorin), Judith Evelyn (Irina Arkadina), Maureen Stapleton (Masha Shamrayen), Montgomery Clift (Constantine Treplieff), Mira Rostova (Nina Zarietchnaya), George Voskovec (Dr. Dorn), Sam Jaffe (Peter Sorin), John Fiedler (Medviedenko), June Walker (Paulina), Will Geer (Shamraeff), Karl Light (Yakov), Sarah Marshall (Cameriera), Lou Polan (Cook).

Appendix 2: Filmography

The Search

1948. *Director:* Fred Zinnemann. *Producer:* Lazar Wechsler. *Screenplay:* Richard Schweitzer.

    Cast: Aline MacMahon (Mrs. Deborah Murray), Ivan Jandl (Karel Malik), Jarmila Novotna (Mrs. Hannah Malik), Montgomery Clift (Sgt. Ralph "Steve" Stevenson), Wendell Corey (Jerry Fisher), Mary Patton (Mrs. Fisher), William Rogers (Tom Fisher), Ewart G. Morrisson (Mr. Crookers), Leopold Borowski (Joel Makowsky), Claude Gambier (Raoul Dubois).

Red River

1948. *Director and Producer:* Howard Hawks. Based on the novel *The Chisholm Trail* by Borden Chase.

    Cast: John Wayne (Tom Dunson), Montgomery Clift (Matthew Garth), Joanne Dru (Tess Millay), Walter Brennan (Groot), Colleen Gray (Fen), John Ireland (Cherry Valance), Noah Beery, Jr. (Buster), Chief Yowlachie (Quo), Harry Carey, Sr. (Melville), Harry Carey, Jr. (Dan Latimer), Mickey Kuhn (Matt, as a child), Paul Fix (Teeler), Hank Worden (Sims), Ivan Parry (Bunk Kenneally), Hal Tagliaferro (Jersen), Dan White (Laredo), Tom Tyler (Quitter), Lane Chandler (Colonel), Glenn Strange (Naylor), Shelley Winters (Dance Hall Girl).

The Heiress

1949. *Director and Producer:* William Wyler. *Screenplay:* Ruth and Augustus Goetz from their play of the same name and from the novel *Washington Square* by Henry James.

    Cast: Olivia de Havilland (Catherine Sloper), Montgomery Clift (Morris

Townsend), Ralph Richardson (Dr. Austin Sloper), Miriam Hopkins (Laviania Penniman), Betty Liney (Mrs. Montgomery), Selena Royale (Elizabeth Almond), Mona Freeman (Marian Almond), Ray Collins (Jefferson Almond), Vanessa Brown (Maria), Paul Lees (Arthur Townsend), Harry Antrim (Mr. Abeel), Russ Conway (Quintus), David Thursby (Geier).

The Big Lift

1950. *Written and Directed by:* George Senton. *Producer:* William Perleberg.
   Cast: Montgomery Clift (Sgt. Danny MacCollough), Paul Douglas (Sgt. Hank Kowalski), Cornell Borchers (Frederica), Bruni Lobel (Gerda), O.E. Hasse (Herr Stieber), Danny Davenport (Private), Fritz Nichlisch (Gunther), Richard O'Malley (AP. Correspondent), Lyford Moore (ABC Correspondent).

A Place in the Sun

1951. *Director and Producer:* George Stevens. *Screenplay:* Michael Wilson and Harry Brown, based on Theodore Dreiser's novel *An American Tragedy*.
   Cast: Montgomery Clift (George Eastman), Elizabeth Taylor (Angela Vickers), Shelley Winters (Alice Tripp), Anne Revere (George's Mother), Raymond Burr (Prosecutor Marlowe), Herbert Heyes (Charles Eastman), Kathryn Givney (Mrs. Charles Eastman), Keefe Brasselle (Earl Eastman), Lois Chartrand (Marcia Eastman), Shepperd Strudwick (Anthony Vickers), Frieda Inescort (Mrs. Vickers), Ian Wolfe (Dr. Wyeland), Fred Clark (Defense Attorney), Douglas Spencer (Boatkeeper), John Ridgley (Coroner), Mary Kent (Landlady), Ted de Corsia (Judge), Paul Frees (Reverend Morrison), Charles Dayton (Kelly).

I Confess

1953. *Director:* Alfred Hitchcock. *Producer:* Sherry Shourdess. *Screenplay:* George Tabori and William Archibald, from Paul Anthelme's play *Our Two Consciences*.
   Cast: Montgomery Clift (Father Michael Logan), Anne Baxter (Ruth Grandfort), Karl Malden (Inspector Larrue), Brian Aherne (Crown Prosecutor Robertson), O.E. Hasse (Otto Keller), Dolly Haas (Alma Keller), Roger Dann (Pierre Grandfort), Charles Andre (Father Millais), Judson Pratt (Policeman Murphy), Ovila Legare (Vilette, the lawyer), Gilles Pelletier (Father Benoit), Nan Boardman (Maid), Henry Corden (Farouche), Carmen Gingras (First Schoolgirl), Renee Hudson (Second Schoolgirl), Albert Godderis (Nightwatchman).

From Here to Eternity

1953. *Director:* Fred Zinnemann. *Producer:* Buddy Adler. *Screenplay:* Daniel Tarandash from the novel of the same name by James Jones.
   Cast: Burt Lancaster (Sgt. Milton Warden), Deborah Kerr (Karen Holmes),

Montgomery Clift (Pvt. Robert Prewitt), Frank Sinatra (Pvt. Angelo Maggio), Donna Reed (Lorene), Ernest Borgnine (Sgt. Fatso Judson), Philip Ober (Capt. Dana Holmes), Jack Warden (Cpl. Buckley), Mickey Shaughnessy (Sgt. Leva), Harry Bellaver (Mazzioli), George Reeves (Sgt. Maylon Stark), John Dennis (Sgt. Ike Galovitch), Tim Rayan (Sgt. Pete Karelsen), Barbara Morrison (Mrs. Kipfer), Kristine Miller (Georgette), Jean Willes (Annette), Arthur Keegan (Treadwell), Claude Akins (Sgt. Baldy Dhom).

Stazione Termini (Indiscretion of an American Wife)

1953. *Director and Producer:* Vittorio De Sica. *Screenplay:* Cesare Zavattini, Luigi Chiarini and Giorgio Prosperi, and dialogue by Truman Capote.

    Cast: Montgomery Clift (Giovanni Doria), Jennifer Jones (Mary Forbes), Richard Beymer (Paul), Gino Cervi (Police Commisariat), Paolo Stoppa (Traveler), Maria Pia Casillo (Bride), Nando Bruno (Baggage Clerk), Celia Matania, Enrico Viarisio, Giuseppe Porelli, Enrico Glori, Memmo Carotenuto, Liliana Gerace, Gigi Reder, Attilio Torelli, Pasquale De Filippo.

Raintree County

1957. *Director:* Edward Dmytryk. *Producer:* David Lewis, *Screenplay:* Millard Kaufman, from the novel of the same name by Ross Lockridge.

    Cast: Montgomery Clift (John Shawnessy), Elizabeth Taylor (Susannah Drake), Eva Marie Saint (Nell Gaither), Nigel Patrick (Professor Stiles), Lee Marvin (Flash Perkins), Rod Taylor (Garwood B. Jones), Agnes Moorehead (Ellen Shawnessy), Walter Abel (T.D. Shawnessy), Jarma Lewis (Barbara Drake), Tom Drake (Bobby Drake), Rhys Williams (Ezra Gray), Russell Collins (Niles Foster), DeForest Kelley (Southern Official), Dorothy Granger (Madame Gaubert).

The Young Lions

1958. *Director:* Edward Dmytryk. *Producer:* Al Litchman. *Screenplay:* Edward Anhalt, from the novel of the same name by Irwin Shaw.

    Cast: Marlon Brando (Christian Diestl), Montgomery Clift (Noah Ackerman), Dean Martin (Michael Whiteacre), Hope Lange (Hope Plowman), Barbara Rush (Margaret Freemantle), May Britt (Gretchen Hardenberg), Maximilian Schell (Captain Hardenberg), Dora Doll (Simone), Lee Van Cleef (Sgt. Rickett), Francoise (Liliane Montevecchi), Parley Baer (Brant), Arthur Frantz (Lt. Green), Hal Baylor (Pvt. Cowley), Herbert Rudley (Capt. Colclough), John Alderson (Corp. Kraus), Sam Gilman (Pvt. Faber), L.Q. Jones (Pvt. Donnelly), Julien Burton (Pvt. Brailsford), Vaughn Taylor (John Plowman).

Lonelyhearts

1959. *Director:* Vincent J. Donehue. *Producer:* Dore Schary. *Screenplay:* Dore Schary, from the novel *Miss Lonelyhearts* by Nathanael West.

    Cast: Montgomery Clift (Adam White), Robert Ryan (William Shrike),

Myrna Loy (Florence Shrike), Dolores Hart (Justy Sargent), Maureen Stapleton (Fay Doyle), Frank Maxwell (Pat Doyle), Jackie Coogan (Ned Gates), Mike Kellin (Frank Goldsmith), Frank Overton (Mr. Sargent), Don Washbrook (Don Sargent), John Washbrook (Johnny Sargent), Onslow Stevens (Mr. Lassiter), Mary Alan Hokanson (Edna), John Gallaudet (Bartender), Jack Black (Jerry), J.B. Welch (Charlie), Charles Fawcett (Smitty), Dorothy Neumann (Mrs. Cannon), Frank Richards (Tassista).

Suddenly Last Summer

1959. *Director:* Joseph L. Mankiewicz. *Producer:* Sam Spiegel. *Screenplay:* Gore Vidal, from the play by Tennessee Williams.

    Cast: Elizabeth Taylor (Catherine Holly), Montgomery Clift (Dr. John Cukrowicz), Katharine Hepburn (Mrs. Violet Venable), Albert Dekker (Dr. Hockstader), Mercedes McCambridge (Mrs. Holly), Gary Raymond (George Holly), Mavis Villiers (Miss Foxhill), Sheila Robbins (Hockstader's Secretary), Patricia Marmont (Nurse), Joan Young (Suor Felicita), Maria Britneva (Lucy), David Cameron (Young Blond Intern), Roberta Woolley (Patient).

Wild River

1959. *Director and Producer:* Elia Kazan. *Screenplay:* Paul Osborn, based on the novels *Mud on the Stars* by William Bradford and *Dunbar's Cove* by Borden Deal.

    Cast: Montgomery Clift (Chuck Glover), Jo Van Fleet (Ella Garth), Lee Remick (Carol Baldwin), Albert Salmi (F.J. Bailey), Jay C. Flippen (Hamilton Garth), James Westerfield (Cal Garth), Big Jeff Bess (Joe John Garth), Malcolm Atterbury (Sy Moore), Bruce Dern (Jack Roper), Judy Harris (Barbara Baldwin), Jim Menard (Jim Baldwin, Jr.), Jim Steakley (Mayor Tom Maynard), Patricia Perry (Mattie), John Dudley (Todd), Alfred E. Smith (Thompson), Mark Menson (Winters).

The Misfits

1961. *Director:* John Huston. *Producer:* Frank Taylor. *Screenplay:* Arthur Miller from his short story.

    Cast: Clark Gable (Gay Langland), Marilyn Monroe (Roslyn Taber), Montgomery Clift (Perce Howland), Eli Wallach (Guido Delinni), Thelma Ritter (Isabelle Steers), James Barton (Old Man in Bar), Estelle Winwood (Church Lady), Kevin McCarthy (Raymond Taber), Dennis Shaw (Cowboy in Bar), Philip Mitchell (Charles Steers), Walter Ramage (Old Groom), Peggy Barton (Young Bride), J. Lewis Smith (Cowboy), Marietta Tree (Susan), Bobby LaSalle (Bartender), Ryall Bowker (Man in Bar).

Judgment at Nuremberg

1961. *Director and Producer:* Stanley Kramer. *Screenplay:* Abby Mann, from his original story and teleplay.

Cast: Spencer Tracy (Judge Dan Haywood), Burt Lancaster (Ernst Janning), Richard Widmark (Colonel Tad Lawson), Marlene Dietrich (Madame Bertholt), Maximilian Schell (Hans Rolfe), Judy Garland (Irene Hoffman), Montgomery Clift (Rudolf Petersen),William Shatner (Captain Harrison Byers), Alan Baxter (General Merrin), Joseph Bernard (Major Radnitz), Ray Teal (Judge Yves), John Wengraf (Dr. Karl Wieck), Martin Brandt (Friederich Hofstetter), Hans Conried (Spectator), Werner Klemperer (Emil Hahn).

Freud

1962. *Director:* John Huston. *Producer:* Wolfgang Reinhardt. *Screenplay:* Charles Kaufman and Wolfgang Reinhard.

Cast: Montgomery Clift (Sigmund Freud), Susannah York (Cecily Koertner), Larry Parks (Dr. Josef Breuer), Susan Kohner (Martha Freud), Eric Portman (Dr. Theodore Meynert), Eileen Herlie (Frau Ida Koertner), Fernand Ledoux (Professor Charcot), David McCallum (Carl von Sclosser), Rosalie Crutchley (Frau Freud), Joseph Furst (Jacob Koertner), Alexander Mango (Babinsky), Leonard Sachs (Brouhardier), Allan Cuthbertson (Wilkie), Moira Redmond (Nora Wimmer), Maria Perschy (Magda), Elizabeth Neumann Viertel (Frau Bernays), Ursula Lyn (Mitzi Freud), Victor Beaumont (Dr. Guber), Manfred Andrea (Student).

The Defector

1966. *Director and Producer:* Raul Levy. *Screenplay:* Robert Guenette and Raoul Levy, based on the novel *The Spy* by Paul Thomas.

Cast: Montgomery Clift (Professor James Bower), Hardy Krüger (Peter Heinzmann), Roddy McDowall (CIA Agent Adams), Macha Meril (Frieda Hoffmann), David Opatoshu (Orlovsky), Christine Delaroche (Ingrid), Hannes Messemer (Dr. Salzner), Karl Lieffen (The Major), Jean-Luc Godard (Orlovsky's Friend).

Appendix 3: Radio Programs, Documentary, Recorded Play

Radio Programs

Broadway and Vine (1948 CBS Radio)
The Cavalcade of America (1951 NBC Radio)
Theatre Guild on the Air (1951 NBC Radio)
Theatre Guild on the Air (1952 NBC Radio)
Stagestruck (1954 CBS Radio)

Documentary

William Faulkner Mississippi (1965)
Director: Don Horan, *Producer:* Robert Guenette, Metropolitan Broadcasting Television. *Narrated by:* Montgomery Clift.

Recorded Play

The Glass Menagerie (1964)
by Tennessee Williams, Caedmon TRS-S301

Notes

ONE: THE LITTLE PRINCE

1. Patricia Bosworth, *Montgomery Clift* (New York: Harcourt Brace Jovanovich, 1978), p. 9.
2. Barney Hoskyns, *Montgomery Clift. Beautiful Loser* (London: Bloomsbury, 1991), p. 22.
3. Robert LaGuardia, *Monty. A Biography of Montgomery Clift* (New York: Arbor House, 1977), p. 10.
4. Myra MacPherson, "Burning Candles for Monty the Hollywood Rebel," *Washington Post,* 6 August, 1979.
5. Bosworth, *Clift,* p. 33.
6. Eleonor Harris, "Montgomery Clift ... Strange Young Man," *McCall's,* January 1957, pp. 70–73.
7. Jesse Zunser, "Monty's Dilemma," *Cue,* 21 September, 1957.
8. Harris, "Montgomery Clift ... Strange Young Man," pp. 70–73.
9. Richard Lockridge, "Fly Away Home. Here After Road Tryouts," *New York World Telegram,* 16 January, 1935, p. 19.
10. Theron Bamberger, "The Children's Corner. Notes on the Young Players Appearing in Fly Away Home," *New York Times,* 27 January, 1935, sec. VIII, p. 2.
11. Bosworth, *Clift,* p. 52.
12. "The Saint Nicholas League," *St. Nicholas Magazine for Boys and Girls,* 8 June 1937, p. 32.
13. Montgomery Clift. Papers, 1933–1966, Produced Scripts, Plays III, box 4, folder 7. Public Library for the Performing Arts at Lincoln Center, New York.
14. LaGuardia, *Monty,* pp. 20–21.
15. Clift, Papers, 1933–1966, Correspondence, I, box 1, folder 4.

Two: Broadway

1. Richard Jr. Watts, *New York Herald Tribune*, 11 January, 1938, p. 14.

2. Clift, Papers, 1933–1966, Correspondence, box 1, folder 8.

3. Judith M. Kass, *The Films of Montgomery Clift* (New Jersey: Citadel Press, 1979), p. 21.

4. Lawrence Langner, *The Magic Curtain* (New York: Dutton, 1951), p. 269.

5. Franklin J. Schaffener, *Worthington Miner: A Directors Guild of America Oral History* (New Jersey: Scarecrow Press, 1985), p. 93.

6. LaGuardia, *Monty*, pp. 25–26.

7. Montgomery Clift, "The Reapers Dance," *Theatre Arts*, March 1939, p. 235.

8. Lehman Engel, *This Bright Day. An Autobiography* (New York: Macmillian, 1974), pp. 108–109.

9. *Ibid*.

10. Lambert Gavin, *Nazimova. A Biography* (New York: Knopf, 1997), pp. 365–366.

11. Sidney B. Whipple, "Mme. Nazimova Appears in an Anti-War Play," *New York World-Telegram*, 26 April, 1939, p. 18.

12. Hoskyns, *Beautiful Loser*, p. 34.

13. Bosworth, *Clift*, p. 73.

14. Elwy Yost, *A Saturday Evening with Montgomery Clift* (1984), NBC-TV.

15. John Griffin, *Montgomery Clift. A Biography* (December 14, 1998) A&E Biography Channel.

16. Maurice Zolotow, *Stagestruck. The Romance of Alfred Lunt & Lynn Fontanne* (New York: Harcourt World, 1964), pp. 227–228.

17. Bosworth, *Clift*, p. 76.

18. Jared Brown, *The Fabulous Lunts* (New York: Athenaeum, 1980), p. 290.

19. Robert Guenette, *Montgomery Clift: His Place in the Sun* (1989), video-cassette.

20. Irving Drutman, "Here Is Another Actor Sure the Stage Is His Destiny. Montgomery Clift Spurns Ripe Hollywood Pastures," *New York Herald Tribune*, 16 July, 1944, sec.4, p. 2.

21. Brooks Atkinson, "Robert E. Sherwood's There Shall Be No Night Brings Alfred Lunt and Lynn Fontanne Back to Town in a Drama About Finland's Resistance," *New York Times*, 30 April, 1940.

22. John Parker, *Five for Hollywood* (New York: Carol Publishing Group, 1991), p. 9.

23. Donald Windham, interview with author, New York, NY, September 27 1997.

24. Hoskyns, *Beautiful Loser*, p. 39.

25. Bosworth, *Clift*, p. 81.

26. Lyn Tornabene, "Montgomery Clift," *Cosmopolitan*, May 1963, pp. 74–80.

27. Robert Lewis, *Slings and Arrows. Theater in My Life* (New York: Stein and Day, 1984), p. 132.

28. John Bradshaw, *Dreams That Money Can Buy. The Tragic Life of Libby Holman* (New York: Morrow, 1985), p. 214.

29. Robert Lewis, Papers. Correspondence, Kent State University, Dept. of Special Collections and Archive, Kent, Ohio.

30 Brooks Atkinson, "Ramon Naya's Mexican Mural Brings Some People of Vera Cruz to the Fiftieth Floor of a Midtown Skyscraper," *New York Times,* 27 April 1942, p. 19.

31. Milt Machlin, *Libby* (New York: Tower Publications, 1980), p. 304.

32. Hedda Hopper, "Monty's Just Himself," *Chicago Sunday Tribune,* March 26, 1950, sec 6, p. 13.

33. Mira Rostova, telephone conversation with author, New York, NY February 10, 1997.

34. Claudio Masenza, *The Rebels. Montgomery Clift,* 1995, videocassette.

35. Griffin, *Montgomery Clift, A Biography.*

36. Masenza, *The Rebels.*

37. Bosworth, *Clift,* p. 91.

38. Myra MacPherson, "Burning Candles for Montgomery Clift," *Washington Post,* 6 August 1979, p. B1–B3.

39. Bosworth, *Clift,* p. 93.

40. Gilbert Harrison, *The Enthusiast* (New Haven: Ticknor & Fields, 1983), p. 263.

41. Elia Kazan, *A Life* (New York: Knopf, 1988), pp. 205–210.

42. Harrison, *Enthusiast,* p. 225.

43. Clift, Papers, 1933–1966, Correspondence, I, box 1, folder 3.

44. Gilbert Harrison, "The Skin of Whose Teeth," *Saturday Review of Literature,* December 26, 1942, p. 12.

45. Bosworth, *Clift,* p. 96.

46. *Ibid.,* pp. 96–97.

47. Masenza, *The Rebels.*

48. *Ibid.*

49. Bradshaw, *Dreams,* p. 229.

50. Lilian Hellman, *Pentimento. A Book of Portraits* (Boston: Little, Brown, 1973), p. 297.

51. Bosworth, *Clift,* p. 103.

52. Drutman, "Here Is Another Actor," sec. IV p. 2.

53. "New Headliners in Theatre," *Vogue,* July 1944, p. 87.

54. Marlon Brando, *Songs That My Mother Taught Me* (New York: Random House, 1994), p. 156.

55. Ben Bagley, interview with author, New York, NY, 28 September 1997.

56. Robert Garland, "Foxhole in the Parlor Opens at the Booth," *New York Journal-American,* 24 May 1945.

57. Howard Barnes, "A Near-Miss," *New York Herald Tribune,* 24 May 1945.

58. Burton Rascoe, "Foxhole in the Parlor Subtle, Exciting, Touching," *New York World Telegram,* 24 May 1945.

59. Bosworth, *Clift,* p. 109.

60. Harrison, *Enthusiast,* p. 263.

61. Lyle Leverich, *Tom. The Unknown Tennessee Williams* (New York: Crown, 1995), p. 589.

62. Peter Hay, *Broadway Anecdotes* (New York: Oxford University Press, 1989), p. 323.

63. Dutson Rader, *Tennessee. Cry of the Heart* (New York: Doubleday 1985), p. 45.

64. Windham, interview.

65. *Ibid.*

66. *Ibid.*

THREE: HOLLYWOOD

1. Windham, interview.

2. *Ibid.*

3. Masenza, *The Rebels.*

4. Bosworth, *Clift,* p. 117.

5. Karl Malden, *When Do I Start? A Memoir* (New York: Simon & Schuster, 1997), pp. 200–201.

6. Slim Keith, *Slim. Memories of a Rich and Imperfect Life* (New York: Simon & Schuster, 1990), pp. 121–122.

7. Todd McCarthy, *Howard Hawks. The Grey Fox of Hollywood* (New York: Grove Press, 1997), p. 414.

8. Peter Bogdanovich, *Who the Devil Made It* (New York: Knopf, 1997), p. 34.

9. Bagley, interview.

10. Shelley Winters, *Shelley Also Known as Shirley* (New York: Morrow, 1980), p. 162.

11. Bosworth, *Clift,* p. 121.

12. *Ibid.,* p. 147.

13. *Variety,* New York, 14 July 1948.

14. Jim Kitses, "The Rise and Fall of the America West," *Film Comment,* Winter 1970–71, pp. 14–21.

15. Bosley Crowther, "Red River. Horse Opera with Montgomery Clift and John Wayne Opens at Capitol," *New York Times,* 1 October 1948, p. 31.

16. Fred Zinnemann, *An Autobiography. A Life in the Movies* (New York: Scribner's 1982), p. 57.

17. Clift, Papers 1933–1966, Produced Scripts, box 15, folder 5.

18. *Ibid.,* box 16, folder 5.

19. Zinnemann, *Autobiography,* p. 61.

20. LaGuardia, *Monty,* p. 62.

21. *Ibid.*

22. Guenette, *His Place.*

23. "Clift's a Babysitter," *Movie Life,* August 1949, pp. 36–41.

24. Montgomery Clift to Ned Smyth, 17 October 1947, Author's collection.

25. Zinnemann, *Autobiography,* p. 69.

26. Graham McCann, *Rebel Males* (London: Hamish Hamilton, 1991), p. 46.

27. Caryl Rivers, *Aphrodite at Mid-Century. Growing Up Female and Catholic in Postwar America* (New York: Doubleday, 1987), p. 283.

28. Steve Vineberg, *Method Actors. Three Generations of an American Acting Style* (New York: Schirmer, 1991), p. 93.

29. Arthur Miller, *Timebends* (New York: Grove Press, 1987), p. 359.

30. Rostova, interview.

31. Jon Whitcomb, "The Moody Montgomery Clift," *Cosmopolitan,* November 1959, pp. 28–30.

32. Bosworth, *Clift,* p. 139.

33. Shelley Winters, *Shelley II. The Middle of My Century* (New York: Simon & Schuster, 1989), p. 69.

34. Parker, *Five,* p. 25.

35. Elizabeth Taylor, *Elizabeth Taylor. An Informal Memoir* (New York: Harper & Row, 1964), p. 48.

36. Donald Windham, *The Roman Spring of Ms. Alice Toklas* (Verona: Stamperia Valdonega 1987), p. 27.

37. Bosworth, *Clift,* p. 151.

38. "New Male Movie Stars," *Life,* 6 December 1948, pp. 22–24.

39. Jim Fragale, "Montgomery Clift. Part II," *Blueboy,* 1978, pp. 37–38.

40. Jack Hamilton, "Montgomery Clift Glamour Boy in Baggy Pants," *Look,* July 19 1949, pp. 57–61.

41. Bosworth, *Clift,* p. 165.

42. Windham, interview.

43. Winters, *Shelley,* p. 281.

44. Donald Spoto, *A Passion for Life. The Biography of Elizabeth Taylor* (New York: HarperCollins, 1997), p. 64.

45. Bagley, interview.

46. Taylor, *Informal Memoir,* pp. 48, 49.

47. Spoto, *Passion,* p. 64.

48. "Barbara Walters Special for Academy Awards Night," 30 March 1987, ABC TV Network.

49. Kevin Sessum, "Queen Elizabeth," *Poz,* November 1997, p. 74.

50. Bosworth, *Clift,* p. 185.

51. Kass, *Films,* p. 50.

52. "Roman Holiday," *Movie Life,* April 1950, p. 80.

53. Bosworth, *Clift,* p. 192.

54. Franco Zeffirelli, *The Autobiography of Franco Zeffirelli* (New York: Weindfeld & Nicolson, 1984), p. 216.

55. Windham, interview.

56. Montgomery Clift, Papers 1933–1966, Correspondence, box 1 folder 5.

FOUR: STAR

1. LaGuardia, *Monty,* pp. 84–85.

2. Parker, *Five,* p. 39.

3. Windham, interview.

4. Bosworth, *Clift,* p. 196.

5. Bradshaw, *Dreams*, p. 306.

6. *Ibid.*

7. A.H. Weiler, "Dreiser's Novel Makes a Moving Film," *New York Times*, 29 August 1951, p. 20.

8. *The Dallas Morning News*, 8 August 1951, sect. II, p. 6.

9. Masenza, *The Rebels*.

10. Merv Griffin, *Merv. An Autobiography* (New York: Simon & Schuster, 1980), pp. 170–171.

11. Kaiser, *The Gay Metropolis 1940–1966* (New York: Houghton Mifflin, 1997), pp. 113–114.

12. Franklin Macfie, telephone conversation with author, New York, NY, January 7, 1998.

13. Kaiser, *Gay Metropolis*, pp. 113–114.

14. *Ibid.*, pp. 114–115.

15. Richard Christiansen, "A Clift Encounter of a Special Kind? Brother Brooks. Remembers Monty," *Chicago Tribune*, 31 January 1979, sec. V, pp. 1–2.

16. Malden, *When Do I Start?*, p. 229.

17. Donald Spoto, *The Dark Side of Genius. The Life of Alfred Hitchcock* (New York: Ballantine, 1984), p. 361.

18. Griffin, *Merv*, p. 172.

19. Spoto, *Hitchcock*, p. 362.

20. Bogdanovich, *Who the Devil*, p. 519.

21. Spoto, *Hitchcock*, p. 362.

22. Malden, *When Do I Start?*, p. 233.

23. Vittorio De Sica, "Gli anni più belli della mia Vita. Faró ancora l'attore per pagare i miei film," *Tempo* vol. XVI, sec. 52, 30 December 1954, pp. 52–54.

24. Bosworth, *Clift*, p. 245.

25. Gerald Clark, *Capote. A Biography* (New York: Ballantine, 1981), p. 235.

26. Montgomery Clift Papers 1933–1966, Produced Scripts, box 11, folder 7.

27. Kass, *Films*, p. 58.

28. Charles Thomas Samuels, *Encountering Directors* (New York: Putnam's, 1972), p. 155.

29. De Sica, "Anni," p. 54.

FIVE: PERTURBED SPIRIT

1. James Jones, Papers, Yale University Library, New Haven, CT, box 34, folder 488.

2. Zinnemann, *Autobiography*, p. 122.

3. LaGuardia, *Monty*, p. 104.

4. Duke Helfand, "Stirring Old Ghosts Amid the Hallowed Haunts of Hollywood," *Los Angeles Times*, 28 October 1995.

5. Robert Windler, *Burt Lancaster* (New York: St. Martin Press, 1984), pp. 76–78.

6. Kitty Kelley, *His Way. The Unauthorized Biography of Frank Sinatra* (New York: Bantam, 1986), pp. 183–185.

7. *Hy Gardner Show,* WOR-TV, New York, 13 January 1963.

8. Bosworth, *Clift,* p. 259.

9. Frank MacShane, *The Life of James Jones* (Boston: Houghton Mifflin, 1985), p. 131.

10. Hoskyns, *Beautiful Loser,* p. 113.

11. Randy Taraborrelli, *Sinatra. Behind the Legend* (New Jersey: Birch Lane Press, 1997), p. 159.

12. Parker, *Five,* p. 64.

13. John Gilmore, *Live Fast — Die Young* (New York: Thunder Mouth Press, 1997), pp. 220–221.

14. Hoskyns, *Beautiful Loser,* p. 114.

15. Bosworth, *Clift,* p. 261.

16. John Howlett, *James Dean. A Biography* (London: Plexus Publishing, 1975), p. 72.

17. Norris Houghton, *Entrances & Exits. A Life In and Out of the Theater* (New York: Limelight Editions, 1991), p. 241.

18. Maureen Stapleton, *A Hell of a Life. An Autobiography* (New York: Simon & Schuster, 1995), p. 69.

19. Rostova, interview.

20. Aaron Weingarten, "Chekhov and the American Director" (Ph.D. diss., the City University of New York, 1972), p. 185.

21. Engel, *This Bright Day,* pp. 111–112.

22. Mike Wallace, *Stagestruck,* CBS Radio, New York, 29 April 1954.

23. Guenette, *His Place.*

24. Anthony Haden-Guest, "Montgomery Clift's Last Interview," *New York World Journal-Tribune,* 20 November 1966, p. 26.

25. Marjorie Stengel, interview with author, New York, NY, 22 February 1998.

26. *Ibid.*

27. *Ibid.*

28. Masenza, *The Rebels.*

29. Robert Thom, "Montgomery Clift. A Small Place in the Sun," *Esquire,* March 1967, p. 154.

30. Truman Capote, *Answered Prayers* (New York: Plume Book, 1988), pp. 103–109.

31. Lewis Mumford Papers 1905–1987, Correspondence, I, box 11, folder 922, Annemberg Rare Book & Manuscript Library, University of Pennsylvania, Philadelphia.

32. Harrison, *The Enthusiast,* p. 263.

33. Paolo Mereghetti, *Dizionario dei Film 1996* (Milan: Baldini & Castoldi, 1996), p. 41.

SIX: TRAGIC DESTINY

1. Masenza, *The Rebels.*

2. Taylor, *Elizabeth,* pp. 56–58.

3. Gardner, *Hy Gardner Show.*

4. Masenza, *The Rebels.*

5. Christopher Isherwood, *Diaries 1939–1960* (New York: HarperCollins 1997), p. 648.

6. Griffin, *Merv*, pp. 213–214.

7. Adele Mailer, *The Last Party. Scenes from My Life with Norman Mailer* (New York: Barricade Books, 1997), pp. 296–297.

8. Peter Manso, *Brando. The Biography* (New York: Hyperion, 1994), p. 447.

9. *Ibid.*, p. 448.

10. Rex Reed, "Charlton Heston," *Daily News,* 15 July 1979, p. 10.

11. Bosworth, *Clift,* pp. 316–317.

12. *Ibid.*

13. Stengel, interview.

14. Karen Swenson, *Greta Garbo. A Life Apart* (New York: Scribner's, 1997), p. 512.

Seven: Changes

1. Edward Dmytryk, *It Is a Hell of a Life But Not a Bad Living* (New York: New York Times Books, 1978), pp. 101–102.

2. Hoskyns, *Beautiful Loser,* p. 142.

3. Nick Tosches, Dino. *Living High in the Dirty Business of Dreams* (New York: Dell, 1992), p. 311.

4. Manso, *Brando,* p. 453.

5. *Ibid.*, p. 458.

6. Bosworth, *Clift,* p. 319.

7. Maurice Leonard, *Montgomery Clift* (London: Hodder & Stoughton, 1997), p. 212.

8. Montgomery Clift, Papers 1933–1966, Correspondence, box 1.

9. Raymond Sarlot, *Life at the Marmot. Now the Walls Talk* (New York: Pine, 1985).

10. "Talk with a Star," *Newsweek,* 7 April 1958, p. 99.

11. Bosley Crowther, "Screen. Irwing Shaw's Young Lions," *New York Times,* 3 April 1958, p. 23.

12. Tornabene, "Montgomery Clift," p. 77.

13. Bosworth, *Clift,* p. 324.

14. LaGuardia, *Monty,* pp. 195–196.

15. Dore Schary, *Heyday. An Autobiography* (Boston: Little, Brown, 1979), p. 319.

16. Stapleton, *Hell of a Life,* p. 151.

17. *Mysteries and Scandals in Hollywood* (May 1998), E! TV Channel.

18. Parker, *Five,* p. 169.

19. Myrna Loy, *Myrna Loy. Being and Becoming* (New York: Knopf, 1987), p. 286.

20. Goffredo Fofi, *Più stelle che in cielo* (Rome: Edizioni e/o, 1995), p. 141.

21. Stengel, interview.

22. Donald Windham, *Lost Friendship* (New York: Morrow, 1986), p. 66.

23. Vernon Scott, "Clift Puts Heart Soul into Roles," *World Telegram,* September 1958.

24. Stengel, interview.

25. Leonard, *Montgomery Clift,* pp. 1–30.

26. LaGuardia, *Monty,* p. 200.

27. Anne Edwards, *A Remarkable Woman. A Biography of Katharine Hepburn* (New York: Morrow, 1985), p. 314.

28. Boze Hadleigh, *The Lavender Screen* (New Jersey: Citadel, 1993), p. 25.

29. Edwards, *A Remarkable Woman,* p. 315.

30. Mercedes McCambridge, *The Quality of Mercy* (New York: New York Times Books, 1991), pp. 217–218.

31. Eddie Fisher, *My Life, My Loves. Eddie Fisher* (New York: Harper & Row, 1981), p. 164.

32. Nigel Berkeley, *National Enquirer,* London 14 June 1959.

33. Roderick Mann, "Interview with Montgomery Clift," *Sunday Express,* 16 August 1959.

34. Edwards, *A Remarkable Woman,* p. 317.

35. Parker, *Five,* p. 175.

36. Kazan, *A Life,* p. 600.

37. Masenza, *The Rebels.*

38. LaGuardia, *Monty,* p. 215.

39. Kazan, *A Life,* pp. 600–601.

40. Gardner, *Hy Gardner Show.*

41. Stengel, interview.

EIGHT: JOHN HUSTON

1. Cleaves Henderson, "The Misfits Fit for Montgomery Clift," *World Telegram-Sun,* 8 February 1961.

2. Arthur Miller, *Timebends,* p. 463.

3. Thom, "A Small Place in the Sun," p. 154.

4. John Huston, *An Open Book* (New York: Knopf, 1980), p. 287.

5. Bob Thomas, "Clift a Success Going Own Way," *New York Telegram-Sun,* 14 November 1960, p. 17.

6. W.J. Weatherby, *Conversations with Marilyn* (New York: Mason Charter, 1976), p. 173.

7. *Ibid.,* 75.

8. *Ibid.,* 146.

9. Parker, *Five,* pp. 188–189.

10. Bosworth, *Clift,* p. 355.

11. Leonard, *Montgomery Clift,* p. 42.

12. Joe Hyams, "Montgomery Clift's Goal Directing," *New York Herald Tribune,* 21 November 1960.

13. "Something Missing," *Newsweek,* 6 February 1961.

14. Paul V. Beckley, "Graphic Reality in Miller's Film," *New York Herald Tribune,* 5 February 1961, sec. IV, p. 10.

15. Guenette, *His Place in the Sun.*

16. Eugene Archer, "Clift Spurns Ray for Right Role," *New York Times,* 7 January 1961, p. 12.

17. Stanley Kramer, *A Mad Mad Mad Mad World* (New York: Harcourt & Brace 1997), pp. 183–184.

18. Christopher Andersen, *An Affair to Remember* (New York: Morrow, 1997), p. 276.

19. LaGuardia, *Monty,* p. 227.

20. Christopher Finch, *Rainbow. The Stormy Life of Judy Garland* (New York: Grosset Dunlap, 1975), p. 217.

21. Thom, "A Small Place in the Sun," p. 156.

22. MacPherson, "Burning Candles."

23. Huston, *An Open Book,* p. 294.

24. *Ibid.,* pp. 299–300.

25. Tornabene, "Montgomery Clift," p. 80.

26. Huston, *An Open Book,* p. 300.

27. Masenza, *The Rebels.*

28. Huston, *An Open Book,* p. 301.

29. Tornabene, "Montgomery Clift," p. 80.

30. Huston, *An Open Book,* p. 300.

31. *Ibid.,* p. 302.

32. *Ibid.*

33. *Ibid.,* p. 305.

34. Lena Pepitone, interview with author, New York, NY, 1 March 1997.

35. Tornabene, "Montgomery Clift," p. 76.

36. Bosworth, *Clift,* p. 395.

37. *Ibid.* p. 376.

38. *Ibid.,* p. 386.

39. Parker, *Five,* pp. 224–225.

NINE: OBLIVION

1. Ralph Zucker, "BackStage," July 1966.

2. Bosworth, *Clift,* p. 389.

3. Thom, "Small Place in the Sun," p. 154.

4. Clarke *Capote,* p. 237.

5. Thom, "Small Place in the Sun," p. 155.

6. Dorothy Levy, *Fire Island News,* 18 June 1977.

7. Bagley, interview.

8. *Ibid.*

9. Bosworth, *Clift,* p. 373.

10. Irmgard Gassler, *Montgomery Clift Unvergessen* (Salzburg: Self-published, 1969).

11. Tornabene, "Montgomery Clift," p. 71.

12. Guenette, *His Place in the Sun*.

13. Montgomery Clift Papers, 1933–1966, Correspondence, I, box 1, folder 1.

14. Haden-Guest, "Clift's Last Interview," p. 28.

15. *Ibid*.

16. Bosworth, *Clift*, p. 409.

17. Peter Fearon, Hal Davis, "City's Axed M.E. and Wife Joked Over Clift's Corpse," *New York Post*, 29 July 1983, p. 7.

18. Zeffirelli, *The Autobiography*, p. 216.

19. Melvyn Bragg, *Richard Burton. A Life* (Boston: Little, Brown, 1989), p. 227.

20. Bradshaw, *Dreams*, p. 364.

21. Loy, *Myrna Loy*, p. 291.

22. Vittorio De Sica, "Letter to the Editor," *Times*, 14 August 1966.

Bibliography

Andersen, Christopher. *An Affair to Remember*. New York: Morrow, 1997.
Atkinson, Brooks. *Broadway Scrapbook*. New York: Theater Arts, 1947.
Bergan, Ronald. *Anthony Perkins. A Haunted Life*. London: Little, Brown, 1995.
Bogdanovich, Peter. *Who the Devil Made It*. New York: Knopf, 1997.
Bosworth, Patricia. *Anything Your Little Heart Desires*. New York: Simon & Schuster, 1997.
_____. *Montgomery Clift. A Biography*. New York: Harcourt Brace Jovanovich, 1978.
Bradshaw, Jon. *Dreams That Money Can Buy*. New York: Random House, 1985.
Bragg, Melvyn. *Richard Burton. A Life*. Boston: Little, Brown, 1988.
Brando, Marlon. *Songs My Mother Taught Me*. New York: Random House, 1994.
Brinnin, Malcom John. *Truman Capote. Dear Heart, Old Buddy*. New York: Delacorte, 1981.
Brown, Jared. *The Fabulous Lunts*. New York: Athenaeum, 1980.
Capote, Truman. *Answered Prayers*. New York: Random House, 1987.
Ciment, Gilles. *John Huston*. Paris: Collection Positif-Rivages, 1988.
Clark, Gerald. *Capote. A Biography*. New York: Ballantine, 1981.
Clinch, Minty. *Burt Lancaster*. New York: Stein and Day, 1985.
Cohan, Steven. *Masked Men. Masculinity in the Movies in the 50's*. Indianapolis: University Press, 1997.
Coope, Stephen. *Perspectives on John Huston*. New York: G.K. Hall, 1994.
Darby, Perry Hamilton. *Libby Holman. Body and Soul*. Boston: Little, Brown, 1983.
Davis, Ronald. *The Glamour Factory*. Dallas: Southern Methodist University Press, 1993.
Devlin, Albert. *Conversation with Tennessee Williams*. Jackson: University Press of Mississippi, 1986.
Dmytryk, Edward. *It's a Hell of a Life But Not a Bad Living*. New York: New York Times Books, 1978.
_____. *Odd Man Out. A Memoir of the Hollywood Ten*. Edwardsville: Southern Illinois University Press, 1976.

Edwards, Anne. *A Remarkable Woman. A Biography of Katharine Hepburn.* New York: Morrow, 1985.

Engel, Lehman. *This Bright Day. An Autobiography.* New York: MacMillian, 1974.

Epstein, Edward. *Portrait of Jennifer. A Biography of Jennifer Jones.* New York: Simon & Schuster, 1995.

Everson, William. *Love in the Film.* New Jersey: Citadel Press, 1979.

Fagen, Herb. *Duke We Are Glad We Knew You.* New Jersey: Birch Lane Press Book, 1996.

Farber, Stephen. *Hollywood on the Couch.* New York: Morrow, 1993.

Fernandez, Luis. *Monty Clift. Pasion Secreta.* Barcelona: Laertes, 1989.

Finch, Christopher. *Rainbow. The Stormy Life of Judy Garland.* New York: Grosset Dunlap, 1975.

Fisher, Eddie. *Eddie. My Life, My Loves.* New York: Harper & Row, 1981.

Fishgall, Gary. *Against Type: The Biography of Burt Lancaster.* New York: Scribner's, 1995.

Fofi, Goffredo. *Più stelle che in cielo.* Roma: e/o, 1995.

Fox, Sheinwold Patricia. *Too Young to Die.* New York: Ottenheimer, 1979.

Friedrich, Otto. *City of Nets. A Portrait of Hollywood in the 40's.* New York: Harper & Row, 1986.

Garrett, George. *James Jones.* New York: Harcourt Brace, 1984.

Gassler, Irmgard. *Montgomery Clift Unvergessen.* Salzburg: Self-published, 1969.

Gavin, Lambert. *Nazimova. A Biography.* New York: Knopf, 1997.

Giles, James. *James Jones.* Boston: Twayne Publications, 1981.

Gilmore, John. *Live Fast. Die Young.* New York: Thunder Mouth Press, 1997.

Goldstone, Richard. *Thornton Wilder. An Intimate Portrait.* New York: Dutton, 1975.

Graham, Sheila. *Hollywood Revisited.* New York: St. Martin's Press, 1984.

Griffin, Merv. *Merv. An Autobiography.* New York: Simon & Schuster, 1980.

Grobel, Lawrence. *Conversation with Capote.* New York: Nal Books, 1985.

Hadleigh, Boze. *The Lavender Screen.* New Jersey: Citadel, 1993.

Hamblett, Charles. *The Hollywood Cage.* New York: Hart Publishing Company, 1969.

Hammen, Scott. *John Huston.* Boston: Twyne Publications, 1985.

Harrison, Gilbert. *The Enthusiast.* New Haven: Ticknor & Fields, 1983.

Hay, Peter. *Broadway Anecdotes.* New York: Oxford University Press, 1989.

Hellman, Lillian. *Pentimento.* Boston: Little, Brown, 1973.

Hoskyns, Barney. *Montgomery Clift. Beautiful Loser.* London: Bloomsbury, 1991.

Houghton, Norris. *Entrances & Exits.* New York: Limelight Editions, 1991.

Housman, John. *Front and Center.* New York: Simon & Schuster, 1979.

Howlett, John. *James Dean. A Biography.* London: Plexus, 1975.

Huston, John. *An Open Book.* New York: Knopf, 1980.

Isherwood, Christopher. *Diaries. 1939–1960.* New York: Harper Collins, 1997.

Jones, James. *To Reach the Eternity. The Letters of James Jones.* New York: Random House, 1989.

Kaiser, Charles. *The Gay Metropolis 1940–1996.* New York: Houghton Mifflin, 1997.

Kalfatovic, Mary. *Montgomery Clift. A Bio-Bibliography.* Westport: Greenwood Press, 1994.

Kashfi Brando, Anna. *Brando for Breakfast.* New York: Crown, 1979.

Kass, Judith. *The Films of Montgomery Clift.* New Jersey: Citadel Press, 1979.

Kazan, Elia. *A Life*. New York: Knopf, 1988.

Keith, Slim. *Slim. Memories of a Rich and Imperfect Life*. New York: Simon & Schuster, 1990.

Kelley, Kitty. *His Way. Frank Sinatra. An Unauthorized Biography*. New York: Simon & Schuster, 1986.

Kramer, Stanley. *A Mad, Mad, Mad, Mad World*. New York: Harcourt Brace, 1997.

LaGuardia Robert. *Monty. A Biography of Montgomery Clift*. New York: Arbor House, 1977.

Langner, Lawrence. *The Magic Curtain*. New York: Dutton, 1951.

Lawrence, Greg. *Dance with Demons. The Life of Jerome Robbins*. New York: Putnam, 2001.

Leonard, Maurice. *Montgomery Clift*. London: Hodder & Stoughton, 1997.

Leverich, Lyle. *Tom. The Unknown Tennessee Williams*. New York: Crown, 1995.

Lewis, Robert. *Slings and Arrows*. New York: Stein & Day, 1984.

Little, Stuart. *Off Broadway. The Prophetic Theater*. New York; Coward McCann & Geoghegan, 1972.

LoBrutto, Vincent. *Stanley Kubrick*. New York: Donald Fine Books, 1997.

Loy, Myrna. *Myrna Loy. Being and Becoming*. New York: Knopf, 1987.

McCambridge, Mercedes. *The Quality of Mercy. An Autobiography*. New York: New York Times Books, 1991.

McCann, Graham. *Rebel Males*. London: Hamish Hamilton, 1991.

McCarthy, Todd. *Howard Hawks. The Grey Fox of Hollywood*. New York: Grove Press, 1997.

McDowall, Roddy. *Double Exposure*. New York: Delacorte, 1966.

Machlin, Milt. *Libby*. New York: Tower Books, 1980.

MacShane, Frank. *The Life of James Jones*. Boston: Houghton Mifflin, 1985.

Mailer, Adele. *The Last Party: Scenes from My Life with Norman Mailer*. New York: Barricade, 1997.

Malden, Karl. *When Do I Start?* New York: Simon & Schuster, 1997.

Manso, Peter. *Brando. The Biography*. New York: Hyperion, 1994.

_____. *Mailer. His Life and Times*. New York: Simon & Schuster, 1985.

Mellen, Joan. *Big Bad Wolves. Masculinity in the American Films*. New York: Pantheon, 1977.

Mereghetti, Paolo. *Dizionario dei film 1996*. Milan: Baldini & Castoldi, 1996

Merigeau, Pascal. *Mankiewicz*. Paris: Denoel, 1993.

Miccichè, Lino. *De Sica*. Venice: Marsilio Editori, 1992.

Miller, Arthur. *Timebends. A Life*. New York: Grove Press, 1987.

Morella, Joe, Epstein, Edward. *Rebels. The Rebel Hero in Films*. New Jersey: Citadel Press, 1971.

Nathan, George Jean. *The Theatre Book of 1943–44*. New York: Knopf, 1944.

Neibaur, James. *Tough Guy. The American Movie Macho*. North Carolina: McFarland & Company, 1989.

Parker, John. *Five for Hollywood*. New York: Carol Publishing Group, 1991.

Parrish, James Robert. *The Great Western Pictures*. New Jersey: Scarecrow Press, 1976.

Peary, Danny. *Close Ups*. New York: Workman Publishing, 1978.

Pepitone, Lena. *Marilyn Confidential*. New York: Simon & Schuster, 1979.

Price, Theodore. *Hitchcock e l'omosessualità*. Milan: Ubulibri, 1995.

Rader, Dutson. *Tennessee. Cry of the Heart*. New York: Doubleday, 1985.

Rivers, Caryl. *Aphrodite at Mid-Century*. New York: Doubleday, 1972.

Samuels, Charles Thomas. *Encountering Directors*. New York: Putnam, 1972.

Schary, Dore. *Heyday. An Autobiography*. Boston: Little, Brown, 1979.

Schickel, Richard. *Brando. A Life in Our Times*. New York: Athenaeum, 1991.

Silvester, Christopher. *The Book of Interviews*. New York: Norton, 1996.

Simon, Linda. *Thornton Wilder. His World*. New York: Doubleday, 1979.

Spoto, Donald. *The Dark Side of Genius. The Life of Alfred Hitchcock*. New York: Ballantine, 1984.

_____. *A Passion for Life. The Biography of Elizabeth Taylor*. New York: Harper Collins, 1995.

Stapleton, Maureen. *A Hell of a Life. An Autobiography*. New York: Simon & Schuster, 1995.

Swenson, Karen. *Greta Garbo. A Life Apart*. New York: Scribner's, 1997.

Taraborrelli, Randy. *Sinatra. Behind the Legend*. New Jersey: Birch Lane Press, 1997.

Taylor, Elizabeth. *Elizabeth Taylor. An Informal Memoir*. New York: Harper and Row, 1964.

Tosches, Nick. *Dino. Living High in the Dirty Business of Dreams*. New York: Dell, 1992.

Truffaut, François. *Hitchcock*. New York: Simon & Schuster, 1967.

Tyler, Parker. *Screening the Sexes. Homosexuality in the Movies*. New York: Holt, Rinehart & Winston, 1972.

Vidal, Gore. *Palimpsest. A Memoir*. New York: Random House, 1995.

Vineberg, Steve. *Method Actors*. New York: Schirmer Books, 1991.

Walker, Alexander. *Stardom. The Hollywood Phenomenon*. New York: Stein and Day, 1970.

Weatherby, W.J. *Conversation with Marilyn*. New York: Mason Charter, 1976.

Weingarten, Aaron. "Chekhov and the American Director." Ph.D. diss., City University of New York, 1972.

Williams, Tennessee. *Letters of Tennessee Williams to Maria St. Just. 1948–1982*. New York: Knopf, 1990.

_____. *Memoirs*. New York: Doubleday, 1972.

Wills, Garry. *John Wayne's America*. New York: Simon & Schuster, 1997.

Windham, Donald. *Lost Friendships, A Memoir of Truman Capote*. New York: Morrow, 1987.

_____. *Tennessee Williams Letters*. Athens: University of Georgia Press, 1996.

Windler, Robert. *Burt Lancaster*. New York: St. Martin's Press, 1984.

Winters, Shelley. *Shelley Also Known as Shirley*. New York: Morrow, 1980.

_____. *Shelley II. The Middle of My Century*. New York: Simon & Schuster, 1989.

Zeffirelli, Franco. *The Autobiography of Franco Zeffirelli*. New York: Weidenfeld & Nicolson, 1986.

Zinnemann, Fred. *An Autobiography*. New York: Scribner's, 1992.

Zolotow, Maurice. *Stagestruck. The Romance of Alfred Lunt & Lynn Fontanne*. New York: Harcourt World, 1964.